The Theatrical Designs of
George Grosz

Studies in the Fine Arts
The Avant-Garde, No. 22

Stephen C. Foster, Series Editor

Associate Professor of Art History
University of Iowa

Other Titles in This Series

The Theatrical Designs of
George Grosz

by
Andrew DeShong

UMI RESEARCH PRESS
Ann Arbor, Michigan

Produced and distributed by
UMI Research Press
an imprint of
University Microfilms International
Ann Arbor, Michigan 48106

Library of Congress Cataloging in Publication Data

DeShong, Andrew.
The theatrical designs of George Grosz.

(Studies in fine arts. Avant-garde ; no. 22)
Revision of thesis (Ph.D.)–Yale University, 1970.
Bibliography: p.
Includes index.
1. Grosz, George, 1893-1959. 2. Theaters–Germany–
Stage-setting and scenery. 3. Theater–Germany–History–
20th century. I. Title. II. Series: Studies in the fine arts.
Avant-garde ; no. 22.

PN2658.G66D4 1982   792'.025'0924   82-1939
ISBN 0-8357-1298-2   AACR2

PN
2658
G66
D4
1982

Contents

List of Plates

"Beg to Report, Sir ... ", lithograph, *Schwejk*

38. Bach, costume design, *Der Kandidat*

39. The Young Count Rheydt, costume, *Der Kandidat*

40. Russek's house and Zum Lamm, *Der Kandidat*

41. The Outlaws, *Grischa*

42. von Lychow and Captain, costume design, *Grischa*

43. Posnanski's office, *Grischa*

44. Willie the Weeper as Saxophonist, *Bilderbogen aus Amerika*

45. Wolf, from Little Red Riding Hood, *Bilderbogen aus Amerika*

Preface

Mention of George Grosz's name evokes a cast of characters from his graphic folios of the twenties: the blustering military man, the smug middle class paterfamilias, the vulgar war profiteer. Grosz's biting satirical drawings brought him early fame, but his contemporaries also knew Grosz as a stage designer who collaborated with the Weimar Republic's great theatrical talents: men like Piscator, Brecht, Pallenberg, Heartfield. In his parallel—but now largely forgotten—theatrical career, the artist George Grosz employed that cast, familiar to us from his graphic work, of character types that he had observed and made distinctively his own. His theatre designs betray feelings similar to the familiar paintings and prints.

In all, Grosz designed only a dozen productions. Nine of these were staged during the first dozen years of the Weimar Republic's short life.[1] Two of the shows he designed were never actually produced with his designs.[2] The twelfth, after World War II, provided a reminiscence of his antic days in the Weimar period and a bridge with his adopted home in the United States.[3] All the designs will be examined in this work.

It may seem surprising that Grosz became widely known for so few productions, but museums exhibited his designs and authors reproduced his sketches during the twenties. Grosz's scenography was exhibited at the great theatre exhibition at Magdeburg in 1927[4] and reproduced in such standard international tomes on modern theatrical design as those by Fuerst and Hume[5] and Moussinac[6], as well as in less popular volumes on German theatre, such as Fischel's[7] and Bab's[8]. Several chronologies of his work have been published.[9] A recent book[10] includes a table of the "two hundred most significant productions on German-language stages" for the revolutionary period 1900–1933. Of this select two hundred, Grosz designed three.

Although the actual designs were sequestered for three decades, ideas that Grosz and his collaborators experimented with in the twenties survived and flourished. A Broadway musical, like *Annie*, uses conveyor belts to move scenery and performers in a fashion similar to those in *Schwejk* designed by Grosz, but the dark comic sensibility which animated the performance four decades earlier is lost. Use of projections in innumerable modern stagings—and particularly in the "avant garde" Czech presentations of the nineteen sixties—is an outgrowth of the techniques with which Grosz and Piscator experimented. The designs and accounts of individual performances discussed in the following chapters will illustrate development of a unique comic sensibility, not easily duplicated, and of innovative design techniques whose descendents we see frequently today.

After Grosz's death in 1959, the contents of an old sketch box were revealed; inside was the treasure of his theatrical designs. The Grosz Estate retained most; a few were scattered to museums and private collectors. The Institut für Theaterwissenschaft in Cologne already owned a substantial number, a legacy from Carl Niessen. Other designs found their way to the Museum of Modern Art where I studied and catalogued them.[11] A small number of these were exhibited at the Busch-Reisinger Museum at Harvard subsequently.

It is rare good fortune to find so concentrated a body of theatrical design. Usually the theatre historian examines designs which are blueprints or diagrams for the way scenery will eventually be made, or a second instance, sketches made after the performance which are records of the stage picture at a given moment. In the case of a portion of the Grosz designs, we are looking at "on stage" participants. These drawings were photographed and then projected during the play. They provide an unusually vivid reentry into the drama of the Weimar period. Looking at them is comparable to holding an actual stage property which can reawaken the spirit of the lost performance.

Comedy has always been a means of overcoming prohibitions, but in the Weimar Republic an almost unique set of social circumstances modified the nature of comedy. At the close of World War I the democratic form of government was abruptly and artificially grafted onto a society which retained imperial Germany's values and traditions. The new republic provided unaccustomed freedoms. Artists were permitted a modicum of freedom to attack the residual society. Grosz and the group of theatre workers about him found many things to oppose: political repression, unemployment, inflation, militarism, conservative modes, and social regimentation retained from Wilhemine days. The freedom granted was legalistic rather than a widespread tolerance of the population toward dissent. Grosz and other artists continually tested the boundaries of their freedom, sometimes with disastrous results and legal skirmishes. When Grosz was prosecuted for obscenity in connection with the publication of *Ecce Homo* in 1923, the prosecution was based on Paragraph 184, a law which dated from 1871. The partial exchange of Wilhemine Germany's codes and censorship for somewhat less restrictive ones did not produce, by itself, the modification in comedy. Factors such as the change in social class of people who attended the theatre were important. More fundamental still, the change in comedy reflected an embittered but humorous percipience born of the theatre workers' experiences during World War I. The common suffering and reaction that Grosz and his generation underwent are treated in Chapter 1.

Several of the comedies Grosz designed end in death, a contradiction in terminology by the standards of other periods. Caricature and several varieties of satire, touched on in Chapter 1, are the basis for Grosz's comic technique. Dada humor, particularly the performer's attack on his audience outlined in Chapter 2, had enormous impact on the comic aesthetic of Grosz's generation. This aggressive stance toward the audience, character-istic of Dada events, continued to appear in more conventional per-formances long after the Dada movement of the World War I years and early twenties had dispersed. A significant number of the plays Grosz designed deal with the death of a rebel-protagonist. By extension, the audience is castigated for allowing the revolution to fail. Grosz and his collaborators had seen the Communist revolution in Germany fail at the close of World War I. Although Grosz's own allegiance to the Communist party may have flagged as early as 1923, he continued to side with the rebel against the ruling class. The death of the rebel will be illustrated in discussion of Georg Kaiser's plays in Chapter 4, in Iwan Goll's *Methusalem* in Chapter 5, and in the *Schwejk* adaptation in Chapter 6. The death of the rebel also animates Toller's serious expressionist play, *Transfiguration*, for which Grosz began designs that were never realized by the director-producer Piscator (Chapter 6). The new absurdist and political comedies, like *Methusalem* and *Schwejk*, contrast with the more traditional, even tepid satires of George Bernard Shaw that Grosz designed (Chapter 3). By conventional literary standards, these dozen plays bear little relation to one another. The choice of plays by a repertory company might similarly seem disparate, but usually careful examination will reveal a consistency in the choice and staging. Grosz's sensibility unites these plays and imposes parallels in staging.

Joy in collaboration, appeal of the political and social themes, and occasionally even remuneration may have prompted Grosz to design these plays. Whatever his reasons, he also responded to the plays. He did so with a comic sensibility closely related to that found in the body of his work. At the core of that sensibility lies anger. Frustrated with his inability to transform the world about him, he reports on that world. Although aware of the socially acceptable view, he rejects superficial appearances, and his eyes fix upon grotesque details and juxtapositions. Power and helplessness are the extremities in which the sensibility fluctuates. Grosz's precise line compen-sates for the powerlessness he feels concerning society. The power struggle Grosz felt is illustrated by the nakedness of his subject-victims, whose shelter and clothing become transparent. Ridiculous vantage and montage effects heighten the sense of absurdity. Iwan Goll's prophetic definition of absurdist dramaturgy will be treated in Chapter 5: Grosz's use of visual non sequiturs was as highly developed as Goll's use of inverted logic and verbal non sequiturs. Another aspect of Grosz's perception is a syncopation, a rhythm achieved within the drawings which seems to reflect the urban tempo of Berlin in the twenties. Even when his ostensible subject is not crime, street fighting, political assassination, or sexual sado-masochism, violence lurks just beneath the surface. Grosz's visual aesthetic correlates with the angry comic aesthetic that developed in Weimar Germany. Weimar's most talented playwrights rejected the distributory justice of melodrama at the same time they avoided the idea of tragedy. The notion of tragedy with its incomprehensible higher beings in control would have been politically defeating to the playwrights of the Left. Grosz's desire to bring about political reform and to report on the existing society led him to choose popular art forms: print portfolios whose mass distribution challenged traditional elitism, and the theatre, where ideas might reach a mass audience. The rejection of traditional "high art" was as important to Grosz as his apprehensive embrace of the masses. What follows is an attempt to trace the birth of a comic sensibility and its manifestations in the theatrical work.

This book is a revision of my doctoral dissertation written in 1970 for the department of Theatre History at Yale University. Where the original format permitted, I have tried to incorporate references and facts from the many recent publications about Grosz and his collaborators. I would like to reiterate my thanks to those who helped with the preparation of the dissertation and to acknowledge the great help of two friends with this revision: Robert Owen and Heide Quittenbaum Chipp.

1

The Saddest Man in Europe

You clamourous world, you Lunapark
You blessed chamber of abnormality,
Attention! Here comes Grosz,
The saddest man in Europe[1]

Grosz's biography is a fascinating tale, although it may be claimed that the story has been told frequently enough. Here the emphasis will be on his experiences which relate in some fashion to theatre. Ironic humor animates every page of his autobiography, *A Little Yes and a Big No*,[2] and our principal complaint must be that Grosz has written more about his times than himself, and that there are frequent lacunae where information is omitted that might have been compromising, particularly politically. Just as Grosz had to write about his era, anyone writing about Grosz must also deal with political and social events. It might be possible to write a biography of important designers, such as Gordon Craig or Adolphe Appia, and to say very little about the impingements of political history upon them. Their indifference to the political world often isolated them in times of crisis. Not so with Grosz, who continually involved himself in the arena of events. Even when he abandoned overt political statements, his natural inclination to redress social injustice pulled his art back to the social-political arena. Grosz's antimilitary caricatures were not just anitmilitaristic philosophy, they were editorials on the actual events which took place in Weimar Germany, open military and paramilitary rearmament after the Treaty of Versailles. The responsive relationship between his work and events holds true in Grosz's theatrical career also, and for this reason this study will occasionally swerve to provide relevant historical information. The primary concern is to examine Grosz's life as it related to theatre.

Neither in art nor in politics was Grosz's highest concern for consistency. His life falls easily into two major periods related to geography: 1893–1933, when he lived in Germany and primarily Berlin; and his immigration to America from 1933 until the early fifties, when he traveled between West Germany and the United States. This second period will be treated in the final chapter. During the first period he moved from the Far Left to a more moderate position; similarly he went from Dada to a style strongly influenced by Cubism, primitive art, and expressionism shorn of its lyrical and humanitarian associations, to Constructivism and on to a social realism in the loosely defined movement dubbed New Objectivity. Grosz could—and did—revert to earlier styles in his art and beliefs.

Grosz's Life and the Theatre

Grosz's father, the manager of a provincial Free Mason's Lodge, died when the artist was still a boy; the family left Pomerania for a brief visit to Berlin, then returned to Stolp. Some of Grosz's early drawings have been kept and reveal a precocious talent exploring such boyish interests as Belling's hussars, scenes of naval action at Port Arthur, etc. Other interests, more pertinent to his future theatrical activity, were the painted displays arranged in booths at provincial fairs. Viewers peeped through holes in the booth's cloth walls to thrill to large canvasses illuminated from below by candles or gas lamps. The subject matter of these painted sensations frequently combined modernity with horror in scenes such as a fire in the Parisian metro. Years later, Grosz compared the illusionism of these murals with the easy acceptance won by modern movies for their outlandish fantasies, in both cases despite the most obvious conventions. He wrote in 1946, "All that we have experienced today as gruesome reality seems to have been antici- pated in these horror pictures."[3] Grosz may have found the models for the officers in *Grischa* in the gentlemen at the officer's club where his mother worked after his father's death. His taste for the grotesque must also have been awakened by the sideshows in which freaks were exhibited within painted canvas walls. Grosz also wrote of his interest in the circus. Along with the painted dioramas and freak shows, the circus provided his earliest impressions of theatre.

In 1909, at the age of 16, Grosz went off to the Royal Saxon Academy at Dresden. He was a rebellious adolescent and had already been in trouble with authorities at the *Oberrealschule*. His great ambition was to paint the huge historical canvasses that were still fashionable in provincial Germany, and he very nearly had the misfortune to achieve his ideal while studying composition with Prof. Raphael Wehle. Even in Dresden students knew the latest mode: Expressionism. Teachers hurled vituperation on "daubs" by painters, such as Nolde; the students greatly enjoyed such conflict. The characteristic art nouveau line and arabesque composition mark several of the drawings and cartoons from this period, when Grosz also experimented with less stylized sketches of genre scenes and drawings of groups of unemployed men standing about. If the setting were lovely and peaceful at Dresden, it could not long rival Berlin's crass and exciting allure. Grosz transferred to the Royal Arts and Crafts School in 1912. He studied under Emil Orlik, a gifted draftsman, who combined qualities of Lautrec and Daumier in his vivid characterizations. He was also, probably, the first designer of stage productions whom Grosz knew. No record remains, but it seems probable that Orlik as well as Count Harry Kessler may have furnished a link between John Heartfield, George Grosz, and the Reinhardt enterprises. It was also in Orlik's class that Grosz met the woman who was to be his wife, Eva. Although he later professed disappointment in Paris, Grosz traveled there in 1913; he met Jules Pascin and became friends. Grosz admired the French artist's drawings of sexual encounters, and these frank statements may have inspired his own uninhibited sexual imagery.

Years later Grosz was to say, during the invasion of the Ruhr, that Berlin's river Spree and not the Rhine was his "front." Ever since Constantin Guys, the portrayal of modernity has been connected with representation of urban life, and Grosz was destined to record the frenetic pace of Berlin. Prosperity which had begun to mushroom after the Franco-Prussian War soon made Berlin the liveliest of German towns. The demise of Munich as a center for the arts, along with other less important provincial cities, did not become an unavoidable fact until after World War I, but already at the turn of the century Berlin was bustling and growing, marked by exciting nightlife and sometimes architectural atrocities. By the twenties Berlin would be irresistible; in it the Rome of Suetonius was combined with Babylon, or so a number of tourists felt. Before World War I, Grosz's marked tendency to role-playing or posing, which Ruth Berenson and Norbert Muhlen have commented on,[4] manifested itself in outlandish dress and powdered face. Walter Mehring, a longtime friend, described the unusual coat and white makeup which formed Grosz's disguise when the political lyricist and dramatist met Grosz shortly after the war:

> . . .I made friends with Grosz, who sat on the terrace of the Cafe Grossenwahn dressed in a loud checked jacket, with face powdered white like a circus clown, posing as the saddest man in Europe.[5]

Grosz merely remarked that he cultivated his distinctive personality. Needless to say, this role-playing was not unrelated to the imaginative abilities a designer must bring to the theatre. Nor was it out of keeping with a general atmosphere of artificiality about him in Berlin. Role-playing, particularly in the antics of the Dadaists to be discussed more fully in the second chapter, was an important part of Grosz's humor in the years to come. Dada pranks suited him admirably. He wore a papier-mâché death's head in place of a hat and twirled a cane with a death's head handle as he strolled along the street.

Berlin was also developing important new industries in the period immediately before and after World War I. Two of these, publishing and moviemaking, offered Grosz his earliest employment. Teachers at the Royal Arts and Crafts school could recommend their students for small jobs. Grosz tried his hand at cartooning for various humor magazines. By 1924, there were 120 newspapers and Grosz drew for many of those on the Left. The burgeoning film industry gave the Berlin theatres, numbering more than 40 by 1924, not counting the scores of cabarets, a troublesome subsidiary that eventually stole the major talents from its parent. During the War, Grosz worked with the brothers Heartfield and Herzfelde on an animated film, "Pierre in St. Nazaire," supposedly a propaganda film about the landing of the Americans in France.

Grosz met John Heartfield in the summer of 1915. About the same time he was making other important and enduring friendshps, such as Piscator's. Like his fellow graphic artist, John Heartfield, whose real name was Helmut Herzfelde, Grosz modified the spelling of his last name *Gross*, and anglicized his first name, *Georg*. Siegfried Kracauer, distinguished drama critic during his Weimar career, has suggested that frequently anglicization of names was based on the fascination which alienated Germans felt with the detective novel.[6] Such novels, with their Sherlock Holmes derivation, were predicated on the liberal society of England, rather than on the repressive social system of Wilhemine Germany. Grosz went beyond changing his name to show his Anglophilia. He frequently followed English or American visitors on the street in prewar Berlin and tried to ape English dress and the casual manners he admired in Americans. Mehring, the Herzfelde brothers, and Grosz seem to have been united by a common sense of humor. Anglophilic charades were a manifestation of its spirit. His friendship with the brothers survived increasing political conflict. Wieland Herzfelde became the publisher of the early Grosz portfolios and some of the later work. Herzfelde's Malik Verlag counted many important Communist writers among its authors.

Heartfield's importance to Grosz's theatrical endeavors can hardly be overstated. He was a direct collaborator on several theatrical projects. With Grosz he pioneered the art and propaganda form of photo montage. Piscator gave Heartfield the credit for inventing "epic theatre" when he arrived late with a backdrop.[7] Grosz claimed credit with Heartfield for the invention of photo montage.[8] Neither claim was entirely serious. Together Grosz and Heartfield brought photo-montage into Dada Art. Heartfield began to design for the Reinhardt theatres under the Hollaender management; he then worked with Piscator, and finally after his return to East Germany after World War II, with Brecht at the Berliner Ensemble.

The friends found one another in the midst of the war. The crucible forming Grosz's generation's spirit was World War I. The war interrupted his modest success as a cartoonist. Grosz served six months as a volunteer, then was dismissed for medical reasons. Accounts of which hospitals he landed in and why vary. Others in his circle of friends had harrowing stories to tell and there was some competitive manufacture of stories of wartime hardships. Toller volunteered; Piscator waited to be called up and then found himself in a special force for entertaining the troops. By 1917 Grosz was back in Berlin, probably having been incarcerated in at least two hospitals and possibly just escaping with life after having attacked an officer.

By the concluding years of the war, the political consensus that had included the Social Democrats was badly damaged. There was no longer cause for optimism; brutality and deprivation disillusioned many. The sense of fraud was reflected in the new Dada publication *Die Pleite*, to which Grosz contributed. Socialists who had expected the proletariat to throw down their arms and halt their machines on realizing that they were battling their class brothers found that the myth was exploded. The gap between the young and the middle-aged was exaggerated beyond all normal proportions. There could scarcely be better field experience for staging *Schwejk, Wandlung,* and *Grischa* than the nightmarish events of trenches, insane ayslums, field hospitals, and prisons that not only Grosz, but many of his generation survived. Similarities in autobiographical accounts by Grosz, Toller, and Piscator are striking and may have been exaggerated to stress their commonality.[9]

Toller pictured the gulf separating two generations sympathetic to one another, that of Max Weber (and Max Reinhardt) and that of Ernst Toller (and George Grosz). The conflict which was mounting concerned the degree and manner of reform once the war was ended:

> With words which endangered life and freedom, Max Weber laid bare the Reich and exposed its evils. The greatest evil seemed to him the Kaiser and he would publicly insult that conceited dilettante until he was forced to take action against him, and then the responsible statesmen, Bülow, Bethman Hollweg, Tirpitz would be compelled to give evidence under oath. Brave words, but they made it clear what separated us from him. We were concerned with more than reforming the franchise. We wanted to create a whole new world, believing that to change the existing order would be also to change the hearts of men.[10]

The idealism of Toller's revolutionary views became identified with the Expressionist movement in literature and received the tag *"O Mensch!"* from his more cynical critics. Nevertheless, the brand of alienation from traditions, the desire for direct action, was also to animate more cynical movements among the young, such as Dadaism. Grosz did not exaggerate the good of the proletariat as Toller did.

While invalided from the war, Heartfield got a job as head of the cartoon and natural science films for a newly formed film company that would later become UFA. Together he and Grosz worked on the animated film which had already been started, "Pierre in St. Nazaire." The importance of the film is, of course, enormous for such concerns as the role of montage in Heartfield's and Grosz's work. More significantly for us, Wieland Herzfelde assured me that it was the entry of both artists into theatre work:

> This had to do with a movie, which the commissioners wanted to use as a propaganda tool for the German war machine, however, it was turned into the contrary by the two artists with the result that it wasn't accepted and naturally never shown. Unfortunately the reel, which my brother kept, was stolen when he was burglarized in the twenties, so practically nothing but memories is left of the film. I myself was present during production as assistant to the camera operator. It was through this work that Grosz and Heartfield came into the theatre.[11]

How curiously appropriate that the creators of *Pierre* were busy undermining the ostensible propaganda purpose of their film in good Dadaist fashion!

During the war, Dada was nurtured in Switzerland. The Herzfelde brothers, Mehring, Grosz, and Piscator quickly joined the Berlin enclave. In addition to friendships and technical innovations, like photo montage, use of lettering, and ambivalent parody of advertising, participation in the Dada movement brought outspoken political commitment. Grosz once succinctly defined Dadaism as the "organized use of insanity to express contempt for a bankrupt world."[12] Grosz, Heartfield, and the "physician Dadaist" Huelsenbeck, who structured the Berlin movement as a political society, were Spartacists, followers of the Soviet-oriented Karl Liebknecht and Rosa Luxemburg, assassinated leaders who became in their followers' eyes martyrs to the repressive White Terror. Liebknecht had been imprisoned in 1916 for his opposition to the War and was not liberated until 1918. He was murdered by the Free Corps—bands of returning soldiers employed by the SPD minister of defense, Noske, to protect the Republic from Communist revolution. The motto of the Spartacus movement was inspired by the Russian Revolution: "All power—legislative, executive and judicial—to the workers' and soldiers' soviets!"

Within the German Dada movement there existed a distinct cleavage between the political and nonpolitical: Kurt Schwitters, for whose collages, frequently made of rubbish, Grosz had only contempt, once wittily halved the German Dadaists into the "kernels" (those, like Schwitters, concerned with formal values) and the "husks", a play on the name of Huelsenbeck, leader of the Dada group in Berlin with its strong political orientation. Ignoring Schwitter's implicit accusation of superficiality, Grosz was solidly aligned with the "husks" in postwar years. Neither the Left not the Right believed in the newly created Republic. Some who had been "a-political", such as Thomas Mann, who so designated himself in the early years of the Republic, became believers too late. Grosz realized years later that he had a deep antipathy to Mann. At the end of 1919, Grosz joined the Communist Party. Sometime after his trip to the USSR in 1922 his allegiance waned. But he continued to work and be friends with dedicated members of the Party until late in his life.

Quickly Grosz set out to be the conscience of the new society. Grosz's patron, the "Red" Count Harry Kessler (it was rumored that he was a natural son of the Kaiser Wilhelm I; he thus maintained considerable influence despite his political views) visited the artist in 1919 and recorded the following impressions:

> ...he sneers at the former ruling classes as accomplices of the gluttonous slothful *bourgeoisie*. He wants to become the German Hogarth ... to preach, improve and reform. ... He has a loathing of traditional painting of the pointlessness of everything that has been done. He is seeking something quite new, or more accurately something which painting once achieved (Hogarth, religious painting) but which was lost in the 19th Century. Reactionary and revolutionary: a symbol of the times.[13]

A symbol of the times is exactly what Grosz made himself in the years immediately after the war and the early twenties. Hannah Arendt has confessed that in her youth the caricatures of Grosz seemed not exaggerations but reportage.[14] In all, the Malik Verlag published 13 portfolios of his graphic work. In these portfolios, as well as in *Der Gegner, Die Pleite, Die Neue Jugend, Jedermann sein eignerfussball*, etc., Grosz attacked moderate and Rightist politicians, the Wilhemine Army, paramilitary rearmament, the polymorphous perversity of Berlin nightlife, the sexual appetites of the middle and upper class Germans, and the inane smugness of the middle class. Three times during the next decade Grosz was tried by Weimar courts: for attacking the Army (1919); for corrupting public morals (1924); and finally, after the publication of *Hintergrund*, a portfolio of lithographs from the drawings used as projections in *Schwejk*, for blasphemy (1928–30). In all but the last case, in which the decision was eventually overturned by a higher court, he lost. Censorship and political imprisonment were not uncommon in Weimar Germany. Toller's plays were censored, although also performed while he remained in prison. Piscator was consistently harassed through the court system. Leading newspapers employed a titular editor who could be sent to jail while the real editors continued to function. The fines, destruction of work, and minor imprisonment in the Weimar days gave way to torture, wholesale destruction of work, and assassination in the Third Reich. Grosz would have been one of the first to be silenced had he remained in Germany later in 1933. He had, already in the Spartacist days, been hidden for a time, and more than once his studio was visited by the paramilitary rightist groups. During the ten years between 1920 and 1930, when Grosz was at the height of his notoriety as an opponent of the ruling classes, he achieved almost all his scene design. In the same time span he passed from the outrageous Dadaism to the Soviet influenced Constructivism and to the New Realism or Objectivity.

The new movement replaced the hopeful idealism of Expressionism and the nihilistic antics of Dadaism. While visual, literary, and theatrical movements do not often proceed at the same velocity or develop on absolutely congruent lines, there is some correspondence between styles in various media. Grosz could, at will, adopt his earlier styles and particularly in theatrical design did so. The New Objectivity in terms of drama meant abandoning dramatic Expressionism's lyrical humanism, the formlessness of many of the sprawling plays, and their lugubriously evocative settings. Based more on pessimism than optimistic aspiration to the brotherhood of man, the new subject was futility and frustration such as that described in Kaiser's plays, treated in Chapter 5, rather than ultimate salvation, as posed in *O Mensch* works, such as Toller's *Wandlung*, discussed in Chapter 6. To those critics who believe that the movement was simply a rebirth of the Naturalism of the eighties and nineties, a glance at the settings for plays produced in both modes would clarify the spirit of the new realism. In the visual arts, the most successful expositors of the new style were Otto Dix and George Grosz. More than coincidence made Grosz the designer of Kaiser's *Nebeneinander*, archetype of the new form of realism in dramatic literature. H. F. Garten describes the historical pressures which molded the style:

> The anarchy of the time, the unsoundness of business enterprise, the harsh contrast between dire poverty and the extravagance of racketeers and crooks form the sordid background of this play: its ultimate message is frustration.[15]

Subject matter of the new realism was close to Grosz's panorama of Berlin in portfolios which followed *Ecce Homo*. In terms of Grosz's own painting and drawing, the influence of the new school meant a somewhat inconsistent abandoning of the cubist picture plane, exchange of nervous jagged line for a more rounded one and a propensity, which was to grow markedly in the next two decades, for old masterly drawing. The most striking thing about this change was its incompleteness: Grosz continued to use the more angular, primitive, and nervous line and cubist spatial techniques when he felt like it. Reality was the observable—the more common or easily at hand the better. The attitude was also a reaction to Expressionism which enjoyed increasing popularity. To an extent the movement was worldwide; in the USSR it became Soviet Realism. In the Depression USA, strong regional movements fostered a realism which resembled many of the German paintings of a few years before. One characteristic was to bring specific areas of subject matter into focus by tight drawing, while the general illusion was disregarded through the painter's inconsistent attention to secondary areas.

The middle twenties not only brought about modification in artistic style, there were also political shifts after Grosz's visit to the Soviet Union where he met Lenin. He continued to work for Communist causes, directors, and publications, but he achieved a greater degree of independence. Grosz's reaction to Soviet Russia was both somatic and emotional: he felt smothered by the repressive atmosphere. This reached a hallucinatory degree when attending a meeting; Grosz felt himself stifled by the thick rugs covering the table around which Bolshevik officials gathered. On the whole, this disillusionment with the Soviets added one more blade to his scalpel. After all, a satirist cannot, if he is a true satirist, put his art at the services of doctrine. The difficulty of being on the offensive and defensive simultaneously is too great. Brecht, after his Marxist conversion, was put into this strange and vulnerable role.

The years Grosz spent in the United States and his return to Berlin after the war are described in the final chapter. Shortly before he died, he was presented with the gold medal of the American Academy of Arts and Letters. As he was giving his acceptance speech, the microphone failed. By one of the curious ironies which plagued his life, he was unintentionally once more the Dadaist clown rather than the distinguished artist. "The audience giggled at his broad gestures: people assumed that the old jokester was doing a parody of the silent movies."[16] A passage from his inaudible address demonstrates how deeply he felt the need to create a lasting art:

> In former days when I essayed political and social satire, I often felt its limitations. In portraying and satirizing the events of the passing scene, the artist is like a fiddler scraping on too small a violin. There is only a small place in great art for the quips and digs and innuendo of the satirist. In all humility I offer you the evidence that I have outgrown the satirical phase of my artistic development.[17]

Satire in Grosz's Work

The "quips and digs" of the satirist may function in a different manner in theatre history than in the history of art or of dramatic literature. Theatre is evanescent and all elements of production share a brief life span of a few hours. Thus satire on stage is not condemned to outlive its moment and its antagonist by imprisonment in a durable form. Hogarth no longer strikes us as truly bitter; he almost seems quaint for the objects of his scorn rarely concern us. In his youth, Grosz astutely recognized the importance of novelty and change in the modern arts; the analysis of his later years may have been less accurate.

Satire's practical effect is generally not in reforming the ills it attacks; rather it sharpens the sense of humor of those who hear and see it. It gives support to opposition. When the smoke cleared from Dada attacks there was a new humor, not a new society. The ground had not been auspicious for traditional forms of satire in Weimar Germany. As Auden has observed, true satire is dependent on a code of conduct shared by satirist and his audience. The society of Weimar Germany provided no such consensus. Grosz, like Goya, was sometimes pushed to the point of crying, "This is not human," rather than lightly underlining a discrepancy between deed and code. Auden sees this set of circumstances as a general characteristic of the twentieth century:

> In an age like our own, it (satire) cannot flourish except in intimate circles as an expression of private feuds; in public life the evils and sufferings are so serious that satire seems trivial and the only possible kind of attack is prophetic denunciation.[18]

It was perhaps this limitation which Grosz felt most keenly when he suggested that the satirist was a violinist playing too small an instrument.

Both Grosz's passion for observed reality, demonstrated in the hundreds of sketch books where he kept hurried notations, as well as his penchant for caricature, served his satire and design for theatre. The tension between recording reality and inventing one as he drew, usually in terms of caricature, is a battle that permeates his entire work, but which becomes crucial in his stage designs. E. H. Gombrich has traced the origins of modern art to their lair in caricature.[19] Even in nineteenth-century caricature, he believes, observed reality is secondary to autonomous creation through playing with line and shape. Gombrich sees the process of caricature as one achieved by assembling traits without fully conscious control. Thus the "automatism" of the modern artist, and the participation of the modern spectator who must in part assemble the image for himself, are brought together by caricature in the manner which has been exploited by the mainstream of twentieth-century art. While Gombrich's notions are a brilliant insight into artistic processes, in the case of Grosz, they must be seen in relation to his penchant for observation. In the more detailed discussion of performances in following chapters, the interaction of Grosz's desire to "editorialize" through caricature and his equally strong desire to make direct reference to observable contemporary reality, economic and social distinctions in dress and furnishings will be shown.

Methods of satire in Grosz's drawings are extremely pertinent to the way in which he designed. Two traditional means of satire formed the basis of Grosz's attacks: the endowment of his subject with qualities of lower animals (the Circe theme is frequent in his work, and in *Schwejk* the jailers are transformed into wolves) and using the outward manifestations of decay and infirmity, such as wrinkles and flabbiness, to symbolize more complicated states of moral decay. Placing his means of satire in categories of a general nature may also help to clarify methods of set and costume design in later chapters. The examples given were chosen for their ability to illustrate the categories, not for particular aesthetic merit, and not from a given period.

First, the most elemental and primitive, might be simple caricature. Caricature is exaggeration with malice. Take, for example, the soldier which appears as "Made in Germany" in *Gott Mit Uns* and which reappears among the drawings for Schwejk projections. He is stupid and repellent in appearance: his bone structure suggests the Neanderthal man; hence the primitive, closer to the animal. The lines are so deft, however, that they certainly provide an aesthetic pleasure distinct from the subject. What is offensive in this sort of attack is its superficiality: people with slit eyes, thick lips, and receding chins are neither universally stupid nor universally evil. In a play, such as *Methusalem*, where Grosz's hostility toward every character was approximately of the same intensity, caricature of this sort could be a brilliant weapon, but in a play such as *Nebeneinander* where Grosz felt greater sympathy with one character than another, the habit of mind could result in uneven editorializing.

A second variety of satire appears over and over again in Grosz's portfolios of prints. The impact of these scenes is an accumulation of details that add up to an environment. It is a technique associated with naturalism. Rather than individual caricature, it is a microcosm of a sinister world: this form of Grosz's satire comes closest to the crowded works of Hogarth, where an accretion of detail provides an environment for his principal characters. Street scenes with a high vantage point, like Breughel's, seem to be populated with mechanical, if evil, dolls. The details of urban life are assembled to denounce man.

In addition to the categories of simple caricature and satire of environment, there might be suggested a third rubric in which the attack is directed more impersonally and most successfully. Satirical allegory brought to perfection by Goya is also used by Grosz. The Death's head, cradling a rifle and wearing a soldier's cap is one of the drawings projected during *Schwejk* (Plate 1). Neither the soldier nor the skeleton is being attacked but something outside the picture: War. The humor is difficult to analyze because we do not laugh. Is it the naive gesture with which Death cradles a now useless gun or the skull's grin that introduces comedy into the figure? In the Constructivist version of *Methusalem* discussed in Chapter 3, Grosz used a similar method to attack a conglomeration of values, symbolized by objects rather than individuals.

In each of these drawings the artist's most telling ingredient is the quality of his line. Line plays a role analogous to the narrator's voice setting tone in fiction. The analogy was exploited in the production of *Schwejk*. Grosz's drawings became a surrogate for the novelist's voice. The projection technique brought line directly on stage, and for this reason *Das trunkene Schiff* and *Schwejk* are Grosz's most successful productions.

2

Antic Preparation

Ragtime blares from the horn of a gramophone. In the foyer of a Berlin studio a skeleton welcomes the visitor. A cadaver, composed of black tights filled with wet salt and topped with a derby, reclines on the sofa. Liquor bottles in the shape of skulls crowd a nearby table. Glasses are similarly formed. A caricature of Hindenburg is propped in one corner. Component parts include a store dummy, a stove pipe, a chamber pot, and a set of grinning false teeth. On the walls are American advertisements for liquor and cigarettes. Autographed pictures of Henry Ford and Rockefeller decorate the studio. One photograph bears the inscription, "In memory of a lurid evening on the bowery with my old friend George, Thomas A. Edison." On leaving, the visitor might be presented with a footsquare calling card 'engraved,' "Dada Field Marshal Grosz"[1]

Dada as Entertainment

To evoke Dadaism by describing its surroundings and props is easier than to define what is less a style than an attitude. The range of stylistic manifestations is broad: from Schwitter's abstract "merz" collages to the pointed messages of John Heartfield's montages, which contain clearly recognizable images and captions. Each artist had his own style, or sometimes several. Attempts to define Dada usually founder in this visual diversity; the range of styles within a movement is not a unique quality of Dadaism, but is found in most post-Futurist movements. If dealing with such variety does not undermine a definition, then the nostalgia of original Dada participants is likely to confuse issues. Some of the characteristics of this movement, particularly as they affected entertainment, are related here because I believe Dada was the major force in shaping a new humor and Grosz's participation in theatre. His disclaiming of Dada in later years, like his retraction of satire and outspoken political belief, must be measured against the impact of the movement on his life. Continuing close friendships with Heartfield, Herzfelde, and Mehring indicated that he was not totally cut off from the world of his youth.

Chronological facts are vital to the spirit of the Dada movement, which relished a sense of its own historical singularity. The historical coincidence which in 1916 placed Lenin's rented room and the Cabaret Voltaire, nursery of Dada, on the same narrow, winding alley in Zurich is an opposition of forces too striking to be ignored. If the architect of the new Soviet order was irritated by noise from the decadent frivolity with which the old order celebrated its destruction, he failed to record his anger. Others were quick to protest, however:

> It began in a small hall with some fifteen or twenty tables and a 100 square feet of stage. The place could hold about 35 to 50 guests. It was packed from the very first evenings. The performances were going strong until late at night, which caused us a good deal of unpleasantness with the neighbours and with the authorities upon the closing hour for public houses.[2]

Zurich was a neutral city crammed with peripheral participants in the war, war-profiteers, and war-weary exiles. Richard Huelsenbeck, the leader of the Berlin Dadaists, thought of the Cabaret Voltaire as an experimental laboratory for the future Dada theatre.[3] On the tiny stage, the similarities of highly individualistic temperaments were stressed. Under these conditions a predilection for "primitive" dances, influenced by Cubist interest in African art, and primitive instruments, which facilitated the improvised dances, emerged. Too much has been written about the destructive force of Dadaism. As already observed, despite its nihilism, the movement actually produced innovative techniques. Hans Richter felt that the spirit of the movement was not destructive, but rather based on artists' attempts to find new solutions to formal problems.[4] What seems apparent is that from the inception, nursed in a cabaret, Dada was closer to entertainment, more evanescent and consciously proud of its transitoriness, than traditional art. It was dependent, too, on its audience. Cubism and Surrealism could be created and appreciated in the semiprivacy of a studio. Without the "shock" effect upon its audience, Dada was missing its mark. As entertainment it warrants definition in terms customarily applied to theatre, the relationship of the performer to his audience, and the nature of the performance. The problem is that our accounts are infrequent and fragmentary and sometimes quite obviously invented, and thus do not warrant generalizations. Of the twelve performances of the Berlin "Club Dada" we possess accounts for only three or so.[5]

The division between performer-artist-Dadaist and his foe, the audience-philistine, was clear in the mind of the Dadaist. Walter Mehring has observed the cleavage:

> From the Dadaist point of view there were two types of people on the face of the earth: on the one side the Dadaist, who saw how funny the madhouse was; and on the other side,

the solid mass of paranoid idiots who thought themselves normal and resented being made fun of.[6]

In theatrical terms, the supreme novelty of Dadaism was the punishment of a nonparticipating audience, a practice which later has been thought to be original, as when Brendan Behan attacked his audience, or the Living Theatre repeated the practice. George Grosz has recounted the pattern which audience-performer relationship followed in the Club Dada:

> I would go out into the audience and say to one man, "You idiot. Pay attention." Sometimes I'd slap them with my glove and sometimes I'd say, "You reek with corruption, and now five hundred marks please."[7]

The attitude of the performer toward his audience was hostility; his method assault; and one goal, in part, no more than self-rewarding fund-raising. The Dadaists discovered a public who would pay to be insulted. Even when the method was less direct, refinements such as simultaneous poetry readings could be interpreted as auditory bombardment. Like many performers before, and many contemporary performers today, the "actors" in Dada performances actually sought self-amusement and self-revelation above enlightenment of their audience. After all, the goal of spiritual trans-formation, the purge of preconceived notions of art, could only be achieved in cases where the audience possessed a rigid view of culture. Henri Béhar has commented on the necessity for this fixed set of values as a foil to the Dada antics.[8]

Most frequently Dada performances were improvised without the spine provided by a dramatic text, which traditionally is considered necessary to theatre. The new principles of the Dada theatre were summed up by Tristan Tzara after the performance of Oskar Kokoschka's *Sphinx und Strohmann* in 1917 at the Galerie Dada.[9] The performance, he felt, was decisive in jettisoning the director in favor of improvisation. The explosive quality of the show was to be ignited by masks and grotesque effects. Accounts of the Swiss and Berlin performances reiterate three characteristics of primary importance: (1) renewed interest in ritual—entertainment which attempts to become participatory rite, (2) spontaneous improvisation—a willingness to incorporate into the most essential parts of the performance not only the response of spectators but also the reaction of performers to physical properties and surroundings, (3) nonsense humor, a willful embrace of the absurd. It can be said, of course, that each of these characteristics can be found in other theatrical performances or even in some degree in all theatre, but it was distinctive to the Dadaists at this point to view these qualities as valid entertainment.

Yearning after shared mysteries or ritualistic performances has usually begun, at least in the twentieth-century theatre, with devaluation or elimination of a literary text. Huelsenbeck, of all the Dadaists, seems to have felt the greatest need for a coupling of negation with collectivity. But the pull toward semireligious experience was not his unique, personal wish. The account, *"Besuch im Cabaret Dada,"*[10] suggests similarities with the semihumorous rituals of the Nabis painters some 30 years before in Paris. Desire for ritual is never divorced in the description from parody. Trappings, such as white fur vestments, a miter, responses, are juxtaposed with bizarre costumes—wigs with peacock feathers, violet underwear, and a conch horn. The audience is invited to join in a candlelit procession and there are responsive gestures and songs, led by the priest-like figure. Dissidents are silenced or expelled. In other words, the collective harmony of the Dada mass will be achieved at any cost.

Desire for ritual was not divorced from improvisation. The surroundings in the preceding description are left rather vague, but the place of performance was always of great importance to the Dada actors. Since the Bourgeois public thought of dramatic art as taking place behind a proscenium arch, the Dadaists took pleasure in shattering such notions by spontaneously performing in almost any locale. The stage of the earlier Cabaret Voltaire, as shown in a painting by Marcel Janco, is merely a low platform around which eager spectators crowd. Later Dada manifestations exploded in private homes, galleries, meeting halls, cabarets, and only occasionally in legitimate theatres.

Adaptability extended to improvising in accordance with costumes created by a single director or invented from materials at hand. The effect of autonomy of masks created by Janco for dances at the Swiss Cabaret has been recorded by Hugo Ball, one of the performers.[11] After the entrance of the creator of the masks, who functioned as stage manager, the masks themselves began to affect their wearers who improvised a "tragic-absurd" dance. The problem posed by the hegemony of costume and mask is an interesting one for all theatre. Once granted that the primary reason for theatre is not the performance of a dramatic text, chaos in the hierarchy of production elements ensues. Why then should not scenery and costumes structure the performance as once a dramatic text offered the spine for a production?

Improvisation, and its more extreme twin, automatism, were carried further by Surrealism, but no movement other than Dada has so consistently relied on humor as a major technique. Nonsense humor, the third of the three chief characteristics, reached an apogee of sorts for the Dadaists in one of the Sunday matinees of the Club Dada in 1919, a performance at the Berlin Charlottenburg Tribune, an avant-garde chamber theatre which had recently begun to play Expressionist pieces. Walter Mehring, poet and political satirist and later author of the *Kaufman von Berlin*, for Piscator, has left us a fragmentary account of the parody of a sporting event in which he and Grosz were the contestants. This entertainment took the form of a race between a sewing machine maneuvered by "Böff" as Grosz was called by his friends, the "World Champion in Procreation and Perforation of Culture" and the diminutive Mehring, "featherweight" manning a typewriter. Volume of noise may have determined the winner. Such "bruitiste" poetry, noises of men doing their best to become machines, and improvised cries in languages unknown to the speakers have been recaptured by Mehring:

> Böff: Schnurre, schnurre-baselurre, (H. C. Anderson)!
> Walt: Tacktacktack! Bumsti! Ping, ping!
> Böff: (Solo on the okarina)-Tulitetut; Luttitu! O sole mio! Old man's river: Mississippi—
> Walt: . . . et Rataplan, rataplan!
> Böff: Wille, wille-wau, wau!
> Walt(aside) -by Wolfgang Goethe!
> Böff and Walt: (in unison) Eiapopeia! Tandara-dei! Hipp, hipp Dada . . . Dada-capo![12]

So successful was the race that the Dadaists decided to hold another matinee the following week. For this performance Mehring chose to recite Goethe's "Wanderers Sturmlied," with the qualm that to deliver a text was "un-Dadaist." Without announcing the author he began to speak the poem; a similar recital had once brought tears to the eyes of the director of his *Gymnasium*. Unfortunately the crowd proved less receptive to Goethe in the improvised form of Mehring's 1919 reading. The entertainment terminated in an exchange of insults: the Dada chorus linked arms and descended from the podium to do battle with the inhabitants of orchestra seats.

The Orestie, einfach klassisch

The physical attack on the audience, improvisational techniques, and desire for collective rites—but not the humor or parody of the Dadaists—were partially set aside in the transition to the Berlin theatre establishment by several members of the Club Dada. This migration in more conventional theatrical haunts had its impact both on the established theatre and upon the Dadaists themselves. It was precisely at the time of the Tribune performances, the ones including the sewing machine race just described, December 1919, that Heartfield, Grosz, and Mehring made their way into Reinhardt's charmed ring where they produced a political puppet play. Neither the creators of the puppet play, the *Orestie*, nor their audience were completely satisfied by the first night. The location of the second "*Schall und Rauch*," Sound and Smoke, a revival of Max Reinhardt's literary cafe, his earliest independent venture which had flourished during the first few years of the century, was appropriate to Dada temperament. The new cabaret was installed in the basement of Reinhardt's "theatre of five thousand," the *Grosse Schauspielhaus*, which actually seated only about three thousand two hundred. This new temple of art sprang up within the shell of an old circus building, the Schumann, where Reinhardt had already staged performances before the war.

The enterprise of the *Grosse Schauspielhaus*, with its central circus ring now modified to a circular apron stage, was of course, another step in Max Reinhardt's experimental quest for the perfect spatial ratio between audience and performance. Despite high hopes occasioned by Reinhardt's return after several years of only intermittent Berlin productions, the new theatre was to prove largely unsuccessful. With increasing political content and control in Berlin theatre, Reinhardt seemed even more the Austrian confectioner to German critics. The very architecture of the new house was an inauspicious blend of Gothic and modern. Hans Poelzig's design attempted to suggest a gothic style with rows of arches arranged in concentric circles and mounting ever higher toward the great central dome. Unfortunately the effect was less architectural than decorative, as if a white fringe had been applied to the auditorium.

Reinhardt chose as an inaugural performance of the enormous new theatre Aeschylus' *Oresteia*, a revival of an earlier, 1910, Reinhardt production of the trilogy in the Zirkus Schumann. Mehring's puppet play, *Orestie*, was presented concurrently in the remodeled basement. Alexander Moissi as Orestes, Werner Krauss as Agamemnon, and Josef Klein as Aegisthus, were generally praised in the reviews of the production on the "main stage." Perhaps the most telling comment on the new theatre's inaugural presentation came from the *Lustige Blätter* which carried a cartoon showing a rotund burgher standing in the center of the apron stage. He placates a vengeful Orestes with the explanation that he has only lost his way while looking for the men's toilet—so much for the integration of audience and playing areas! Fritz Engel noted that while the effect of a player placed in the audience was fine for the orchestra seats, the special sensation of intimacy offered by the new theatre could hardly reach the many galleries.[13] The critics dwelt upon what was new, not the production of the *Oresteia*, but its performance in the new space of the remodeled circus. Most of them found the spirit of the tragedy drowned in technical novelty.

The performance of the cabaret in the cellar offered a kind of anti-masque to the presentation upstairs. The space occupied by tables and stage of the *Schall und Rauch* had been the home of circus animals. Painted in a bright red and green color scheme by the chief of Reinhardt's designers, Ernst Stern, the tunnel-shaped hall had undergone few other improvements and was notably lacking in acoustics and intimacy. The "conference provocative" written by Mehring included a customary Dada consecration of the premises, as well as a few pointed references to the former inhabitants and the animal nature of man. The central metaphors of the evening's entertainment were to be the disorder of the political situation as a circus and men as beasts. The ring leader became the chorus leader in Mehring's text; the verse would require a poet as clever as Mehring to translate it, but the sense goes like this: "The Circus rules, cultures are being destroyed! The beast sneaks forward ready to spring/In the ring's giant earthen circle/Tamed until the next performance!/I step forward in the never fail, heroic pose . . ."[14]

Although the prologue was pronounced the day before the performance, the spirit of both was much the same. The critic for the *Vossische Zeitung* succinctly observed: "Aeschylus above, Aristophanes below." Indeed, it is difficult to write about the entertainment without joining the game initiated by the Dadaists themselves of posing genres to describe the hybrid fun. The evening was staged by the author Rudolf Kurtz, with Heinz Herald acting as a sort of *Dramaturg*. The inaugural, filled with song and dance, set the tone for a cabaret repertory of high quality and strong opposition to military and political reaction.

It is gratifying to note that although the performance was flawed in the eyes of both critics and creators, almost all of the latter went on to fame or greater fame while the former are pretty much forgotten. Lyrics and verse for the premiere were written by Walter Mehring, Klabund, and Kurt Tucholsky, one of the editors of the prestigious *Weltbühne*, writing under the name of "Theobald Tiger." Entertainers included Blandine Ebinger and Paul Graetz, who received the greatest ovation of the evening for his recital of political satire written in verse by Tucholsky. Friedrich Hollaender, best known to Americans as the composer of naughty and haunting melodies sung by another cabaret artist of the period, Marlene Dietrich, as well as music for many films, composed several songs and music for the puppet show. A film, an animated cartoon in grafitti style, portrayed a day in the life of the President of the Reich. President Ebert was to suffer further criticism before the evening was over. After the film came the final number of the variety program, the puppet play which had been advertised as the main attraction. George Grosz designed the marionettes in collaboration with John Heartfield and with the assistance of Waldemar Hecker, a veteran of the earlier satirical cabaret, the *Elf Scharfrichter*. The subject of the satire was a modernized, inverted, and rather convoluted parody of the *Oresteia*, only tangentially following the lines of the tragedy. The author slyly worked in a reference to the satyr play of antiquity, believed to have been a comic reworking of the tragic material of the preceding trilogy: "According to ancient custom, the heroic mess of a miserable tragedy was once again followed by a malicious satyrical farce . . ."[15]

Events of the previous months had provided sufficient mess, "Kladderadatsch," as Mehring called it, raw material for countless satires. Nineteen-

nineteen was the year the German Federal Republic emerged from the chaos of a defeated and badly divided nation, from a society which could not find trained leadership among newly elevated classes nor rely upon the old and inefficient leadership of the former regime. The eventful year began with a new federal constitution and a National Assembly, progressed to the Spartacus revolt, then the Bavarian uprising following the assassination of Premier Eisner and the temporary Munich Soviet headed by Toller. The signing of the Versailles Peace Treaty, an act for which no party wished to assume responsibility, took place in the summer of 1919. Repugnant admission of guilt, dangerously unspecific reparations eventually to be balanced against an overwhelming national debt, and the deprivation of territories which had been German, were secondary to the symbolic value of the humiliating treaty. Conditions for signing were to become the basis for fantasies of vengeance and for the spread of the myth that Germany had not been defeated militarily but betrayed by the republican revolution.

The political free-for-all was mirrored in theatre by a growing tendency toward political commitment. The new political theatre was not purely a reaction to the need to take sides in political debate, which verged on civil war. The political tinge of most productions was also a reaction to the lifting of Wilhelm's throttling censorship during war years. Piscator started his first theatre, Das Tribunal, in Königsberg. Karl Heinz Martin promulgated a political program at the Tribune and Leopold Jessner took over what had been a royal playhouse to do his famous *Tell*, rigged out in modern dress on a stark stage, to become the prototype of Jessner's trademark "*Treppen.*" Brecht reacted to the Spartacus revolt by writing *Drums in the Night*.

Various obstacles which might have prevented a first night altogether seem only to have contributed to the feverish disorganization of the evening. As the show took place during one of the year's several general strikes, patrons arrived on foot or by beer wagon. Hollaender has explained that street fighting might have been impaired if the beer industry had been forced to halt. Electrical service had been interrupted so part of the performance was illuminated by candles. How the animated film got through this is not recorded. A row of candles formed the footlights and others flickered on tables.

Sadly neither the complete text nor a reliable synopsis of the puppet play is available. The through story line was often obscured in satirical skirmishes. In the first section there were numerous attacks and quips at the expense of the army, with lots of double meanings. A not very accurate sample (because slang as well as double meanings spice Mehring's verse) "Our army lives Spartan, and in bars, Pompeian, Pull the ordinary lever, and drop grenades on Spreeathens (Berlin)." An oratory on War, Peace, and Inflation, recounted the sufferings of the German people from 1914 to 1918 tracing the deflating spirits of the population and inflating economic crisis:

"But in the year of the hail 1918, it so happened that the generals spoke: The party is lost! Therefore the citizens ran to the enemy begging, 'Peace!' Then the Navy, and the whole army revolted: 'Hand us the culprit' But the gentlemen talked and answered no more."[16]

The second half of the play was called "dawn of democracy." The inconsistencies and ineffectuality of the Weimar Republic were personified in the figure of Pres. Ebert, a trade unionist, who many felt had betrayed his class in becoming president of a republic which made the transition from Wilhemine artistocracy to democracy with difficulty. Grosz wrote in 1946:

> Ebert, the former saddle-maker now president of the Republic was occupied with having his moustache cut just so, so that he could look like the executive of a large corporation. Instead of wearing the hat of the democrats of 1848, he wore a tophat. He had a part to play. Meissner, the Privy Counsellor, the master of Ceremonies of the Republic, saw to it that Ebert did everything according to court etiquette and nothing to reveal the well known fact that he had once been of the proletariat.[17]

Above all, Ebert had suppressed the Spartacists, but in the next half decade he would coddle the Right. Aegisthus/Ebert said while training with his punching ball:

> Gentlemen and Ladies! It is easy to laugh.
> But improving, improving!
> By the way, have you ever once reigned?
> (Starts again with heavy punches)
> Pretty soon one's dissected from the Right, then the Left.
> Soon you appear in the morning paper covered with blood,
> Caricatured by Zille in the Supplement
> Inspected, persiflaged and spied upon.
> And yet the romanticism is missing,
> the heroic pose, the gigantic stride
> There's no crown now, one can't sit enthroned,
> In a word: it's no longer worthwhile.[18]

During these pictures of the New Republic, Electra had been transformed into a Salvation Army girl. A film was part of the staging.

The final part satirized the fall of the German monarchy. Orestes became Kaiser Wilhelm II and Oreste's escape, Wilhelm's flight and abdication in Holland.

Friedrich Hollaender has left us a description of the interior of *Schall und Rauch* during the performance of the puppet play.

> Next: the political puppet theatre, again Mehring. Knackfuss accompanies on the grand piano. Everyone accompanies his own piece. Spoliansky is asked to a table, Champagne stands on the table. A Yul Brynner head; Simplicissmus' caricature of a fraternity student suddenly jumps from his chair and bows deeply. The candle is flickering. In the meantime

we perform the puppet play. The audience neighs, nibbling all the personalities like carrots from our hands. Spoliansky makes hand signals. Don't understand a word. Spolli scribbles something on a paper napkin. A waiter tiptoes towards me and puts the napkin on the music stand. Outside another shot cracks. The candles cringe. Spolli gesticulates. Points his index finger at the paper napkin. Yes, I'll get to reading it, right after the next song is finished.[19]

Puppets weren't an unusual form for the Dadaists. The originality of the play was its pointed satire and the caricature with which Grosz and Heartfield had captured well-known types. The surviving designs show that Grosz thought of marionette movement in conventional terms. The dolls or puppets were seen after the show in both Heartfield's and Grosz's studios. Rosemarie Hammer made reconstructions of some of the Heartfield puppets; her reconstructions are 50 to 60 centimeters in height. Their clothing was real cloth and the heads were of papier-mâché, modeled and carefully painted as caricatures of the well-known personalities.[20]

A first impression of these designs is likely to be that we are seeing "Grosztypes," a cast of characters he chose to flay repeatedly and mercilessly. In the sketches the colors are strong and bright—green, blue, orange, and red. Agamemnon, with bald head, bushy eyebrows and jutting jaw and teeth, is the archetype of the Junker general. His short cape and helmet seem to be removable, according to a quick sketch in the upper right. The head of the second Agamemnon is that of the first. The cape is replaced by an officer's great coat with a military collar. His helmet is retained. Grosz's "classical" touches, the classical Greek key design about the collar and hem of the cloak, maintain about the same relationship with antique design that Mehring's text provided with the original *Oresteia*. As Agamemnon (Plate 2) is the comic quintessence of an apoplectic general, so Aegisthus (Plate 3), shown doffing his top hat, is no less an archetype of domesticated and ineffectual bad humor. His top hat, black coat, high collar, rimless pince-nez and pink and white striped "kilt" contrast with hairy legs protruding from his disarray. He seems vulnerable, contrasted with the General. Other surviving designs include a watchman, who probably played an analagous part to the watchman in *Agamemnon*, and a figure which, though not labeled, probably represents Clytaemnestra. If so, the transformation from Argos to Weimar is even more striking than in the case of the male costumes. She wears a ruffled dress of the sort a can-can dancer might flaunt. Beneath the center split skirt can be seen her yellow and white striped petticoat. Again there are minimal concessions to the antique mode in her headdress and the Greek key design on the hem of her petticoat. From the tips of her yellow boots to her flaming red hair she typifies an interpretation of the regicide as virago. How the "Bourgeois gentleman" and Nature Boy figured in the show remains unknown.

Critical reaction was generally enthusiastic about the cabaret enterprise, particularly as Reinhardt's tacit sponsorship promised a revival of a form of cabaret entertainment that was vanishing before unenlightened vulgarity. The critics of the dailies were reserved in regard to the puppet show, which after all included elements sure to offend both Right and Center. *Freiheit*, a journal of the Social Democrats, praised the general talent, particularly mentioned the hilarity and formlessness of the puppet show, and concluded that the whole was unsatisfactory for its time and public.[21] Another Social Democratic paper, *Vorwärts*, while granting that the Dadaists were just the proper artists to do justice to the madness of contemporary events, spoke of the grotesque effects of figures drawn by Grosz.[22] The review concluded that while the performance might become more polished, its public was unlikely to change. *Berliner Tageblatt* saluted the talent of Mehring in preparing the spicy *Oresteia*. Not everything was new or original, the paper went on, citing the ridicule of his Highness as hackneyed. In conclusion, skipping over aesthetic gaffs, the paper summed up its comments on the evening with a pun on Kurtz's name: "Short and Good."[23] Both the latter newspapers noted the protest lodged by Grosz, Heartfield, and Mehring against the "unprepared and distorted" performance of the puppet show.

While neither conditions of performance nor public could be considered ideal, the Dadaists had at least taken a first step in the conventional theatrical world. In true Dadaist fashion they had succeeded in amusing and provoking their audience and critics. What remains of the text appears antilogical in its mixture of topical references and inverted chronology; the whole must have given an impression of improvisation.

In a sense, turning tragedy into contemporary satire is antiritual. The creators of *Orestie* sought a political solidarity quite distinct from the aesthetic mystic solidarity of the Zurich Dadaists who engaged in primitive dances and music. The Berlin political solidarity was of a small group, critical both of traditional values, such as heroism, and of modern civilization, in part for the absence of such values. In their self-conscious superiority and isolation, they were rather typical of the intellectual critics of the Weimar Republic. Mehring's text and the Heartfield-Grosz puppets provided a more fixed structure than the impromptu devices of earlier Zurich and Berlin performances. The humor had been sufficiently irreverent and absurd to confuse reviewers, but the management of the Reinhardt theatres must have been impressed, for both Grosz and Heartfield began to design settings for more conventional stagings, and did posters for this cabaret. Grosz's cover for the March-April program of *Schall und Rauch* was a typical phantasmagoria of Berlin types. When Piscator sought to eliminate live actors in his production of *Schwejk*, he recalled these grotesque puppets created by Grosz and Heartfield, and with Grosz's help instrumented a solution.[24]

3

Shaw in Shendot and Toga

Grosz's designs for *Caesar and Cleopatra* (Deutsches Theater, 1920) and *Androcles and the Lion* (Residenz Theater, 1924) are properly discussed together. Although a span of four years separated the production dates of the two Shaw plays in period costume designed by Grosz, his drawings are allied spiritually and stylistically and bear some relation to his antique costume for the puppets in *Orestie*. It would also be hard to guess that the designs were accomplished during transitional times for Grosz, a period that saw him moving politically away from Communism and experimenting with Constructivism in his own painting. In designing all three productions, Grosz and his collaborator John Heartfield departed from the primary tradition of late eighteenth- and nineteenth-century stage design—that of archaeological accuracy. They also left behind the new mode of Expressionist scenography which sought a central emotional symbol about which to construct an affective image, the guiding principle of Gordon Craig's designs, which will be examined in relation to his own proposals for a production of *Caesar and Cleopatra* at the Deutsches Theater more than a decade before Grosz's designs.

Good humor marks Grosz's costume and setting drawings for Shaw's plays. His characteristic anger abated. He sought universal comic types, playfulness, and even whimsy. The more gentle tone has led Wolfgang Storch to dismiss the settings as "picture book."[1] Two factors may have brought about the modification in Grosz's temper: his rampant Anglophilia and the tepid social criticism of George Bernard Shaw in these two plays. In general, Shaw's brand of social criticism contrasts with the kind of critique that Grosz and his allies made toward the society of Weimar Germany. Shaw criticized from within the society he attacked. By post World War I standards, his censures are blunted by the indirection of historic setting. His Irish nationality did little to diminish Shaw's involvement in British society. By contrast many of the authors for whom Grosz designed—Goll, Toller, Piscator, Brecht, Zweig, and even Kaiser—maintained a not entirely voluntary aloofness, even alienation, from the society of Weimar Germany. Typically, Shaw inverted and parodied existing dramatic forms rather than inventing. In *Caesar and Cleopatra* and *Androcles* Shaw stood melodrama on its head in a historic setting. While he had insights on recurring historical situations, such as the suppression of a dissident minority (*Androcles*) and the moral contingencies of power (*Caesar*), none of his themes was exactly revolutionary, even for his own era. The audience remained free to evade the allusions to contemporary problems. More successfully, Shaw sought to toy with the existing expectations of his audience, the sort of anticipations brought about by viewing history through the plays of Sardou and nineteenth-century historical pageantry in Shakespearean productions. Shaw deglamorized his hero, but replaced the glamor with a practical energy which triumphed much as preposterous endowments had in Sardou's plays. Since a German audience in the second decade of the twentieth century only rarely found these historical clichés on stage, the major impetus for producing either play might be thought to have evaporated. The movies, however, may have prolonged Shaw's relevancy. A new film genre, which was of course not new at all, but a continuation of nineteenth-century history plays, was beginning to crowd the German screens with extravagant, fairly accurate costumes and splendid settings and improbable heroes and heroines.[2]

Caesar and Cleopatra

Shaw tells two stories in *Caesar and Cleopatra*: Caesar's invasion, conquest, and abandonment of Egypt, and his education of Cleopatra. The action begins with a framing scene in the courtyard of Cleopatra's palace (Plate 4). A group of Egyptian soldiers gather to speculate upon Caesar's arrival and the omen of the missing sacred white cat and the disappearance of their girl queen. In the first scene of the first act Caesar finds the young queen cradled in the lap of the Sphinx. They return to the palace; in the throne room Caesar imparts his first lesson in controlling servants and followers. Cleopatra thus achieves a new and delicious autonomy from her bossy nursemaid Ftatateeta. The second act has only one setting: a room in Ptolemy's palace at Alexandria with a view of the celebrated harbor. Rivalry between Cleopatra and her brother Ptolemy does not deter Caesar in his practical quest for money. More upsetting to him is the return of Lucius, murderer of Pompey, who makes clear, as the dream or ghost would in an Elizabethan play, that Caesar's power and generosity rest on bloody deeds. Caesar defends the island of Pharos and the palace and surroundings from Egyptian troops supporting Ptolemy. While on the quay before the palace Cleopatra purchases a rug from the effete Apollodorus in order to smuggle herself into Caesar's headquarters at Pharos across the harbor. There (III, ii) the rug is hoisted from Apollodorus's boat. Cleopatra emerges from the center of a pile of scarves wrapped in the rug. When the Egyptian queen and her older admirer are threatened with being stranded on the island, first Apollodorus, then Caesar, jumps into the sea. Finally Rufio throws Cleopatra into the water. A year in the womanly transformation of the queen passes unseen between this dunking and our next glimpse of the queen (IV, i). In the interior of Cleopatra's boudoir her musical interlude with the ladies of the court is halted by the conniving Pothinus, who attempts to enlist her aid against Caesar. Her evening banquet with the Romans is again interrupted, to Cleopatra's fury, by Pothinus. He comes to accuse her before Caesar of wanting Caesar out of Egypt. As the dinner terminates on the roof of the palace, a man's death shout rises from below. Having killed Pothinus, Ftatateeta returns to worship at the altar of the god Ra. As the Romans run out to attend to the commotion caused by the murder in the street, Rufio pauses to slit the throat of the praying woman servant. The anticlimactic fifth act takes place in front of the palace on the day of Caesar's departure from Egypt. To Cleopatra's displeasure the soldier Rufio is elevated to governor, while she, grown more womanly and cunning, is appeased by Caesar's promise to send Mark Antony.

In 1906 Reinhardt invited Gordon Craig to design a production of *Caesar and Cleopatra* for the Deutsches Theater, shortly after a too timid production designed by Karl Walser. Craig's designs were eventually rejected by Reinhardt with good reason. Walser's designs had suffered from a cloying affection for the picturesque. Craig's became heavy-handedly emotional, with little appreciation for the comedy he was designing. In *Towards a New Theatre* Craig discusses three of the seven designs he made. Apparent in his chatty comments are annoyance with Shaw's appallingly complete stage directions and a general discomfort with the play. In each of the scenes which Craig designed he exerted himself to find a symbol—visually effective and emotionally affecting—around which he might build a setting. As was his custom, light, particularly great areas of shadow, heightened the drama of the central motif—whether it be the Sphinx, the thrones of Caesar and Cleopatra, or the bars in Craig's metaphor of court as cage. Craig seems troubled by lack of emotional content; many scenes play with conventions and fail to take the stage settings seriously. Craig's interpretation consistently undermined the play. Although it may be argued that one cannot design the play without making some comment, the divergence of Craig's emotional and Grosz's rational comments is striking.

Grosz's lack of respect for the art of the past was a positive advantage in his designs. Unlike Craig, who knew the Sphinx to be too grand and mysterious for the stage, Grosz had no first hand knowledge of the Sphinx. He knew antiquity from the very good Berlin museums. Grosz's lines are as crisp as Shaw's language, and the effect of his settings—when placed alongside Craig's maquettes—is one of streamlined modernity. Clearly defined planes, vivid colors, and strong light show that Grosz did not share

Craig's idea that the "Socialist sphinx" was "splodgy, restless and threaten-ing."[3] On the contrary, he saw it as a clearly delineated sculpture, set at an angle to the footlights and furnishing a humorous foil to the encounter between Caesar and Cleopatra. The theatre historian Franzjosef Janssen may exaggerate the influence of New Objectivity in Grosz designs, but he is on the right track when he points out:

> In the Neue Sachlichkeit of the twenties once again a shift towards reality took place as a reaction to the hectic and deforming style of Expressionism. The aim was to portray the complete world of objects of comprehensible reality with the utmost clarity and non-pathetic objectivity. Examples for achieving this new mode can be found in the set design for Shaw's Caesar and Cleopatra by Grosz . . . any expressive note is missing. Objects are placed in a matter of fact approach to space.[4]

More legitimately matter-of-fact, Grosz's later designs for Kaiser's plays avoided the exotic touches here. It may not have always been the exoticism of Egypt. Wieland Herzfelde goes so far as to report that the harbor of Alexandria reminded him of Scandinavia: "Ancient Egypt was natually recognizable as Egypt through costumes, text, architectural picture, and landscape. But what an Egypt. Being clean and simple with a lot of blue and white, but no gold and smoke, it rather reminded one of a Scandinavian harbor during the best September weather."[5]

Grosz seems to have worked peacefully with Heartfield and been content to accept suggestions from the director Fritz Wendhausen. From the harbor scene maquette to the final version, there is a perceptible alteration to facilitate blocking. In the sketch the back wall parallels the footlights. In the final rendering, the parapet is set obliquely for greater illusionism.

Settings which Grosz designed do not stretch the limits or resources of the stage. They are hardly revolutionary. Rather they employ stock low platforms and set pieces in conjunction with painted flats and backdrops. Although Grosz chose here, as elsewhere, to adopt a high angle of vision (designing for the balcony as it were), the sets do not appear to overpower the comedians. The actor is allowed to move in a pretty, fictitious, and highly ordered world in which he remains paramount.

The real strength of the Grosz-Heartfield designs stems from the integration of settings and comic costumes. Grosz adopted a set of conven-tions of his own manufacture: the Egyptians are shown in the stylized manner of Egyptian wall paintings; the Romans are rendered in an illustrational style, with frequent details which reveal them to be not Romans, but Englishmen. Plaids, woolen fabrics, and duller colors are consistently employed for the Romans, while the Egyptians are generally scantily clad in light fabrics with geometric designs, most frequently stripes.

The importance of historical research was not altogether disparaged. Cleopatra's costume developed from a modern flapper to a parody of an

Egyptian wall painting. In the costumes for the Egyptian women Grosz got his only chance to indulge a taste for the erotic that was frequently cloaked in ambivalent moralizing in the graphic folios.

Much as Shaw used anachronism to remind his audience that he was not presenting the usual nineteenth-century history play, Grosz updated the costumes with details of anachronistic nature. British-Roman soldiers wear mufflers and helmets (Plate 5). Roman soldiers are garbed in a shade of khaki green which suggests World War I camouflage.

In some costumes; that of Apollodorus, for instance, a figure derived from Oscar Wilde (Plate 6), Grosz had a wonderful time in depicting the zenith of fastidious aestheticism: pink shading to mauve, grey tights and high sandals, with emerald green accessories. Among the anonymous supernumeraries sporting gay colors, stripes, and humorous details, several portraits emerge particularized in traditional comic roles. Gesture, facial expression, color, and stylistic detail combine to form comic types. The sketch of Ftatateeta garbed in an enormous blue shawl collar which accentuates her shoulders, bare midriff, Negroid hairdo which suggests the Southern Mammy, broadly striped skirt of white, brown, and red, embodies the invincible loyalty and bossiness of Cleopatra's nursemaid, but also suggests a wider association of types, the savage, the mother-in-law, the virago.

A balding Caesar, still concerned with appearance, stands in the manner of a wrestler. His super-aquiline nose, heavy brows, and body hair give the impression of virility, but the knee length skirt is a bit too long and much too plaid to be taken seriously (Plate 7). These are not the standard types which Grosz normally used. They witness his giving of his imaginative powers to the dramatic text. Although Grosz's Caesar is more a general and less an intellectual than Shaw's, where else in Grosz's work would a general be so sympathetically portrayed as the hard-bitten, energetic Caesar is here?

In production there were frequent modifications of Grosz's designs. Almost every change appears to have been for the worse, a sacrifice of Grosz's humor to expediency. In performance Ftatateeta, played by Tini Senders, wore a great brown sack garment and an elaborate headdress. Such changes may have compensated for the size and physical characteristics of the actress—perhaps also for the prudery of the public. Production photographs also reveal that neither Caesar, played by Werner Krauss, nor Cleopatra, Else Eckersberg, wore costumes for which maquettes remain. Krauss was a different physical type from the Grosz drawings of Caesar; not the tough soldier, rather a younger and fleshier man. Vital distinction between Roman and Egyptian dress was destroyed by the simple but conventional dress worn by Senders.

The cast[6] was assembled from varied backgrounds by Felix Hollaender, who had just become manager of the Reinhardt theatre complex in

Reinhardt's absence. A popularly-held conception of the Reinhardt performers was thus belied. Since the play was given for 57 performances in
1920–21 and in five productions in subsequent years, the actors may have
eventually adjusted to their disparate backgrounds. Werner Krauss, as
Caesar, was an actor who had in 1920 just completed the film *The Cabinet of
Dr. Caligari*, in which he played the insane Dr. Caligari. His earlier triumphs
had been in Expressionist theatre also, but he survived the mode, a durable
star. Else Eckersberg, Cleopatra, was then a young operetta singer with little
training in acting. A versatile actress from Vienna's Burgtheater, Tini
Senders played Ftatateeta. The most famous name in the cast belonged to
the young actor who played the boy king Ptolemy: Peter Eysoldt, son of
Reinhardt's able intellectual actress Gertrud Eysoldt.

Werner Krauss made the only definitive opening night conquest. Most
critics thought that Eckersberg was too shaky, too much the musical comedy
soubrette, for the potentially dangerous Shavian femme fatale Cleopatra.
Senders was praised largely for bulk, though her performance suggested
neither England nor Egypt. Peter Eysoldt and Max Gulstorff, the faithful
Britannus, were applauded for their ability to maintain the Shavian tone.

Popular critics and journals—not the intellectual ones—applauded the
production in general. Paul Wiegler even stated that Fritz Wendhausen, the
director, succeeded where Reinhardt failed. One of the curious conditions of
long established repertory theatre was that critics frequently compared
successes and failures of like-minded theatrical personnel. Although *Caesar
and Cleopatra* had not been mounted by the Deutsches Theater in 15 years,
it was the Reinhardt production of 1905 that served for comparison. Such
distinguished critics as Siegfried Jacobsohn and Herbert Jhering were
extremely reserved in their praise and insisted on their preconceived inter-
pretations of the Shaw play. Jacobsohn had the nerve to quote his own 1906
review extensively. He had not liked the Reinhardt production, finding it
lacking in daring and style. While he granted that Wendhausen had daring,
the style was still absent. Although Grosz was certainly an integral part of
the attempt to make the play relevant to postwar audiences, he was not
mentioned by Jacobsohn. Jhering was sympathetic with attempts to mod-
ernize the play and with an attempt to integrate Shaw's verbal wit and the
somewhat crude "knock-about," such as Cleopatra's concealment in the rug
and Caesar's dive into the harbor by means of a frantic pace. He concluded
that Wendhausen had seen a means of solving the problem without really
achieving the solution. Jhering was an important dissenter to the general
praise which Grosz-Heartfield settings and costumes received:

> Pace did not create a new style, but encompassed all styles of performance and direction
> since Reinhardt, without their being digested. Despite the fast tempo and vehemence, the
> performance was charged, extemporaneous, the actors interrupted, mumbled and pushed.
> The artistic concept of the director (as well as the designer, the otherwise extraordinary
> draftsman, George Grosz) was missing in this performance.[7]

The magic and parody of theatrical mystery in certain settings, particularly the Sphinx and the courtyard, appealed to reviewers: "The performance at the Deutsches Theater was funny and spirited. The Sphinx stood mightily and ghostly in front of the purple desert horizon, and the lights sparkling from within the head of this mythical animal showed, nevertheless, that one dealt with an enormous magical event," wrote Max Hochdorf in *Vorwärts*.[8] Paul Wiegler in *Die Dame* wrote, "Beautiful and liberated by fantasy are the designs by Grosz and Heartfield, rows of ancestors of Egyptian gods, men with hawk heads and animals of Ra's altar, gently parodied mysteries."[9]

Androcles and the Lion

So close are spirit and style of Grosz's designs for *Androcles* to those of *Caesar and Cleopatra* that they suggest a production proposed earlier than the one performed in 1924 at the Residenz Theater, a large art theatre with 670 seats. The Deutsches Theater where *Caesar* was given accommodated almost twice that number. The intimate scale of *Androcles* made it ideal for chamber productions, and the play was frequently presented in Reinhardt's smaller Kammerspiele, where capacity was only 336.

Shaw was delighted with the frigid reception originally accorded *Androcles* in Germany:

> It was currently reported in the Berlin newspapers that when *Androcles* was first performed in Berlin, the Crown Prince rose and left the house, unable to endure the (I hope) very clear and fair exposition of autocratic Imperialism given by the Roman captain to his Christian prisoners. No English Imperialist was intelligent and earnest enough to do the same in London. If the report is correct, I confirm the logic of the Crown Prince, and am glad to find myself so well understood. But I can assure him that the Empire which served for my model when I wrote *Androcles* was as he is now finding to his cost, much nearer my home than the German one.[10]

Shaw's theme of "prophetic blasphemy" must also have appealed to Grosz. In the light of Grosz's own trial for blasphemy during the suppression of the portfolio *Hintergrund*, drawn from his sketches for *Schwejk*, the theme is ironic. Shaw wrote in 1915:

> . . . but the thing (trial and punishment of blasphemers) is done because the governing classes, provided only the law against blasphemy is not applied to themselves, strongly approve of such persecution because it enables them to represent their own privileges as part of the religion of the country.[11]

There are three settings for this short play: a path in the country, a square on the outskirts of Rome, and finally a passage near the Emperor's box in the coliseum. The timid Greek tailor, Androcles, overcomes his fear and removes a thorn from the lion's paw. His shrewish pagan wife, Maegara, is indignant at the budding amity between Christian and beast, who waltz off together. Androcles next appears in the company of a group of captive Christians, among whom are Lavinia, an unconventional free thinker, Ferrovius, a rash but muscular fighter, and Spintho, whose greatest fear is that he will miss the chance to atone for his sins through martyrdom. He, of course, fulfills this anxiety by blundering into the jaws of a lion outside the arena. Shaw saw Christianity as a revolutionary movement in the context of persecution by the Empire and was quick to observe that revolutions attract men who are both above and below the general level of the society they oppose. The idealism of the potential martyrs is contrasted with the practicality of a pagan Roman captain, in love with Lavinia, and a pair of supercilious and cowardly partricians, Lentellus and Metellus. The latter eventually become Ferrovius's victims when they attempt to torture him. The audience, of course, expects Androcles's friendship with the lion to save the day in some fashion, but the feat is preempted by Ferrovius's un-Christian, but heroic, slaughter of the Roman centurions in the arena. Androcles is selected as scapegoat when it is decided to appease the crowd by offering a Christian. The justification is that this Christian is Greek and probably a sorcerer. The lion recognizes his old friend, but is quite hostile to the Emperor who is only saved through Androcles's Christian admonitions.

While Grosz's maquettes for the settings received numerous changes, his costume designs appear to have been rendered more faithfully than in the case of *Caesar and Cleopatra*. The first scene, the jungle path, is reminiscent of the jungles of Douanier Rousseau with great flattened cubist leaves, about two meters high, filling the stage, both hanging and as ground rows. The second decor, on the outskirts of Rome, is more routine: a drop of rolling hills, broadly painted marble steps and low platforms, a sign pointing to Rome. The hand is characteristic of twentieth-century advertising and the only touch that is particularly Grosz's. (Herzfelde incorrectly reproduces this scene as one from *Caesar and Cleopatra*; the setting doesn't fit that play and neither do the costumes.)[12] On Grosz's sketch the annotation reads: "Second act. Background very naturalistic, pale yellowish white marble type arch, see detailed sketch." The detailed sketch has disappeared and why Grosz wanted the drop of rolling hills to be naturalistic after his patterned and improbable leaves in the first scene is not clear. For the final act, the spectator almost joins the emperor in his box. There are two basic levels: the stage floor and a platform about seven feet above the floor. Various steps and lower platforms connect the two principal levels. A central portal beneath the higher platform affords an entrance to the prime center, downstage area. The great arch in the background is vaguely suggestive of the larger structure of the coliseum.

As in the case of *Caesar and Cleopatra* these settings would be no more than adequately amusing without the addition of Grosz's costumes. Whereas he had used color to distinguish opposing civilizations in *Caesar*, he did not use repetitive schemes in designing *Androcles*. A whirl of bright color belies the potential martyrdom of the Christians. Some of the details of the costumes for the two plays are strikingly similar: Caesar's plaid kilt and Rufio's muffler are echoed in the plaid kilt and muffler of the Captain (Plate 8). He is obviously a British soldier masquerading as a Roman, from monocle to service decorations. Lavinia's costume was more demure in production than Grosz's original design in which her toga is rakishly draped from one shoulder. Megara wore a large violet gown, cut like a modern evening dress, and a short cape with enormous purple dots. The call boy wears a pink toga, bright green sandals, and a green cap in Grosz's sketch. The editor (referee) (Plate 9) is nattily attired in yellow sandals and shoulder pads, black arm band, white silk scarf, and short flaring skirt. He is the quintessential dandy-athlete. Grosz's costumes for the keeper, call boy, and editor make *explicit* the *tacit* satire on British sportsmanship by Shaw. As in the costumes for *Caesar*, Grosz's ability to create designs with specific details of a comic nature, such as the oversize whistle of the editor or Androcles's enormous peasant hat, while simultaneously suggesting a broad range of comic types, accounts for much of the visual success of the production.

The director, Robert Pirk, was not a particularly distinguished member of the Rotter enterprises. The Rotter Brothers, somewhat in the mold of the Shuberts, were primarily interested in boulevard productions with stars. Julius Bab characterizes the Rotters in unflattering terms:

> They produced, as a rule, mediocre society plays by Sudermann or by French authors, though now and then an intrinsically valuable literary work. They always employed the most piquant stars possible, used a stage setting of the most shameless pomposity, presented an ensemble carelessly and cheaply jumbled together; but above all they made their way by means of an advertising machinery so shameless and so tasteless that in other times it would have been restricted to the marketing of tainted herrings.[13]

He goes on to note that the greater the economic inflation, the more successful the Rotters' escapist fare; since inflation was epidemic in 1923–24, the Rotters were at the top of the heap with a dozen theatres in Berlin and more in the provinces. (It should be noted that the Rotters closed their theatres immediately when the Third Reich was proclaimed). The antipathy to rampantly commercial production was one reason that intellectual journals and critics ignored the *Androcles* production. Another reason was that intellectual reviewers sought new productions and avoided revivals of plays frequently seen. The same year, the Rotters took over the Central Theatre from Piscator, who moved to the Volksbühne. Reinhardt returned to direct *The Servant of Two Masters*. Iwan Goll's *Methusalem* finally received its premier. Brecht was in Berlin as *Dramaturg* to the Reinhardt theatres.

Most of the actors in *Androcles* were Rotters regulars,[14] but this did not necessarily mean that they were inferior craftsmen. Paul Biensfeldt, who played Androcles, had made his debut with Otto Brahm's Deutsches Theater and remained to appear under Max Reinhardt's direction. Franziska Kinz (Kasebach) was also a member of the Reinhardt stages over a period of time, beginning in 1922. Hubert von Meyerinck, the Captain, although he was not the original Mackheath, went on to make that charming antihero of Brecht and Weill one of his principal roles. Biensfeldt was rather a pudgy Androcles, but Kinz and von Meyerinck were typecast for their characters.

The anonymous critic for the *Weltspiegel Anzeigen*, not above suspicion as a paid Rotter tout, reported that the production was one of the best seen at the Residenz. He also praised the "marvellous modern art settings" by George Grosz. *Die Woche* was also impressed with the success of the production. A more knowing reaction came from the critic of the Republican *Vossische Zeitung*, owned by the Ullstein publishing house:

> Shaw at the Residenz Theatre? The audience was amused: it was presented with a fast-paced, light comedy. But was it by Shaw? Well, one has to admit: the script for this performance was by Shaw without any doubt. But his work was not sufficient for the direction (Robert Pirk).[15]

For about three decades Grosz did not design a production so easygoing and free from direct offensiveness. Only in his last ballet designs did Grosz return to the gentler vein of diversionary humor out of which he created *Caesar and Cleopatra* and *Androcles and the Lion*.

4

Methusalem

Dada humor surfaced again in designs that Grosz prepared in 1922 for Iwan Goll's *Methusalem*. Grosz's identity as a Dada Field Marshal had been rather well-concealed in his drawings for Shaw. George Grosz was, after all, a man who could be a Dadaist and preserve many bourgeois values; a man who could be a Communist yet not believe in the masses; and one who called himself a Constructivist but instinctively sought two-dimensional representation. Goll's innovative drama involves elements from all three movements: Dadaism, Communism, and Constructivism. Written in 1921, after the *Caesar* production but before *Androcles*, *Methusalem* provided an important link between the Berlin Dadaists led by Huelsenbeck and the Parisian-Dadaist-Surrealist milieu which had formed about Apollinaire before his untimely death in World War I. By the production date in October 1924, the thrust of Dada was somewhat blunted. Iwan Goll remarked that the presentation came just four years too late when he wrote from Georg Kaiser's Berlin apartment to his wife in Paris:

> I sent you the most important ones: Kerr strangely enough, really wonderful, the *8 Uhr Abendblatt*—which turns me into a Werfel—today follows *Vorwärts* with a hymn, but also the most wonderful vulgarities of the reactionary press, which might be even more amusing to you than *Methusalem* itself. Too bad, Jhering didn't write. Kantor is firm. Overall, I really feel the play has come four years too late: most points appeared to be flat here. Berlin is no longer astonished by anything, it knows all the dirty tricks.[1]

Grosz made two sets of *Methusalem* drawings, in two styles. If one knew only the costume designs in "illustrational" style (Plate 10), one might discern a continuity with the 1920 renderings for Shaw. Grosz reworked the illustrational designs in Constructivist mode (Plates 12–14), exchanging organic forms in the illustrational designs for mechanical shapes in the Constructivist version. We don't know if there were complete sets in each style. In making the change to Constructivist style, Grosz made important changes—both in iconography and spirit—and an idea occurred to him or was suggested by Goll (because of his link with Parisian Dada and interest in masks) which extended the possibilities of the stage. The vision was the total disguising of the actor's face and body, a transformation which would involve the modification of all conventional acting technique. Stylistic unity came close to the ideal in this visionary production. The irony, considering the unusual interest of the designs, is that his ideas of 1922 were never carried out on stage. Critics have often written as if they were.[2] There were, in fact, two productions of *Methusalem*: one in Berlin designed by Hannes Boht, the one in Paris by Medgyès. Production photos make clear that the Berlin staging did not use either set of Grosz's costumes. Both Berlin and Paris saw costumes which resembled the first, and less adventurous, set of Grosz's designs. No mention is made of Grosz or his designs in Iwan Goll's letters from Berlin to his wife in Paris. Both Claire and Iwan Goll were poets and members of international art circles, particularly the Surrealist group in Paris. Their friends included a Who's Who of modern art; artist friends, such as Kokoschka, Léger, and Delaunay frequently illustrated their poems. Grosz illustrated the 1922 volume of *Methusalem* with three watercolors. It is natural then that the playwright's widow insisted that Grosz had actually designed the stage production; as already shown, she was not in Berlin to see the German premiere.

Although written in 1921, Goll's extraordinary play anticipates many techniques of the "absurdist" school, such as non sequiturs in dialogue, as well as theatrical developments, such as the integration of film and stage action. It is unusual in that the play's message ridicules the grotesquerie of the middle class but suggests almost as strongly the absurdity of revolution. In the final scene, when the student has overthrown Methusalem, his shoe factory, and the middle class structure, his new wife Ida, Methusalem's daughter, asks:

> When will the revolution be over?
> Student: When the others no longer have their villas.
> Ida: And when we have one?
> Student: That's when the next revolution begins.[3]

In a play which announces so many innovative techniques influential on later drama, antecedents become unusually important: Strindberg's *A Dream Play* and even more Jarry's *Ubu roi* contributed more than a little to Goll's technique. As in the *Dream Play*, the structure is loose, even episodic, though the story line emerges quite clearly in sequence and there is much that is simply fantastic. The attack on the *Bourgeoisie* is paralleled only in *Ubu roi*. Characters, such as the Student, are much like the generic types which populate Expressionist drama.

The Plot of *Methusalem*

Goll's 10 scenes or episodes retain some logical causation. Although they could not be played out of sequence, they often have a quality of complete vignettes. The play is a parody of the stock events of domestic comedy, such as the separation of young lovers by repressive parents. We are introduced to the middle class Methusalem household in the first scene. While Methusalem, the shoe magnate, reads his newspaper and props up his gouty foot, wife Amalia rattles on in a nonstop string of clichés and non sequiturs. A recurring point is her taste for sensational violence. At the close of the scene, Goll intended that three filmed "dreams" be projected on a screen while Methusalem dozed off in an armchair. In the first of these film clips he speaks intensely to each of the various women in his life—his daughter Ida, Anna the cook, etc: "As in a comic strip a speech balloon flutters out of his mouth, 'Dearest, whoever you may be, wear Methusalem shoes and be true to me. . . .'" He interrupts *Hamlet* during the gravediggers' scene in the next dream. This time the advertisement balloon is: "Drop that nonsense! The dead can fly but man must walk on his feet." In the final dream he is a general leading an enormous parade of boots. He wakes fitfully and places a coin in a metal robot, which then begins to tell racist jokes that greatly entertain the shoe manufacturer. Later in the play this mechanical clown reappears at the death of Methusalem.

The first four scenes take place in Methusalem's house (Plate 11). There are various modifications possible for stage lighting and phantasmagorical effects. A Dada twist animates the second scene: the animals, both pets and stuffed trophies, revolt. They plot the death of Methusalem in manifestos with arguments such as this one put forth by the monkey: "Did a tiger ever have to read Nietszche to be Dionysian? Man is the disgrace of this earth!" Among the rights he demands is, "The right to copulate in the middle of boulevards and avenues without fear of scolding spinsters."[4]

The budding love of Ida, Methusalem's daughter, for her bohemian Student is portrayed in her conversation with Aunt Emmy in the following scene. Next Felix, the scion and heir, appears. He speaks a jargon composed of stockmarket quotations and business news. The megaphone he has in place of a mouth announces a strike at one of Methusalem's shoe factories. The elder Methusalem is naturally alarmed, and through the window the audience sees a street mob approach. The Student, at the head, denounces Methusalem. When Methusalem pushes a button, police appear with drawn revolvers to scatter the crowd. The tableau, demonstrating the power of the shoe king, ends abruptly with a bit of ritual worthy of a monarch from another age:

> As things calm down two servants in gold braid bring in a richly covered commode, help Methusalem unbutton his trousers and take them down and place him upon the stool. The mob is completely mastered, the police stand stiffly, waiting his orders. Methusalem smiles and farts.[5]

An act break facilitates the change of locale from the Methusalems' living room to a park. Goll's stage directions call for three identically masked actors who represent various facets of the Student's mind. When an aspect of his conscious or subconscious is momentarily in ascendance, the I or Thou or He, as is appropriate, steps forward. It's not quite pat Freud. The He lusts; the I urges caution; the Thou echoes Ida's poetic fantasies on a more genuinely poetic plane. Ida is consistently a single identity: a lyrical, if brainless, ingenue.

Goll follows the attempted seduction scene with another from traditional romantic comedy. During the party that follows, it transpires that the Methusalems have other plans for their children than marriage with bohemians. Three couples, friends, arrive; they are exaggerated embodiments of middle class vulgarity. The ladies' hats particularly reveal the tastlessness Goll enjoys hating:

> The women, although middle class, wear extravagant costumes; their hats are a pot of red geraniums, stuffed birds and the Reichstag building in miniature, made of papier-mâché.[6]

The upshot of a great deal of social inanity is that a marriage is almost contracted for Felix with Mr. and Mrs. Katgut's daughter. Negotiations terminate, however, over the cost of vellum for invitations. Methusalem refuses to splurge on such items. "Greed alone leads to wealth," he unabashedly replies to Katgut's jeers. Having muffed this alliance, Methusalem manages to get Ida engaged to their friends, the Heavenlys', son.

Next a blithely lyric Ida announces her pregnancy. The inevitable outcome is that Felix must defend the family honor with a duel against the Student. A wedding, with comic knock-about disputes, interrupts the duel in the park. When Felix shoots the Student he triumphs over his spiritual nature alone, as embodied in a winter overcoat:

> He shoots. The Student falls immediately. The exhalation of his soul is visible in the form of a winter overcoat which leaves him and floats off into the distance. Immediately thereafter the Student gets up again.[7]

Returning to the Methusalem house, he interrupts a rendezvous between the cocotte, Veronica, and her would-be lover, Methusalem. This time the revolution, complete with a crowd carrying banners of Liebknecht and Luxemburg, is successful, despite Methusalem's passionate address to the mob, "Liebknecht always wore Toreador Shoes!" The Student shoots Methusalem. The members of his family assemble to express grief in thoroughly predictable attitudes: annoyance at the interruption of their daily routine. In the final scene, Ida and the Student are once more in a park, now accompanied by their brat, little Godfrey. Their boredom is undisturbed even by the return of Methusalem, who appears to be just what the play's subtitle indicates: the eternal burgher. He is concerned, as usual, with his business, the weather, and his goulash. Since Goll twice employs the regeneration of a character, in Methusalem and the Student, he underscores a point about the absurdity of revolution: *"plus ça change . . ."*

Proposed Settings and Costumes

Grosz designed the settings, and presumably the costumes also, with Goll's advice. We can be sure about the settings because of one of his frequent annotations. This one, on the *Ich-Du-Er* design reads, "the same actor (Student) always in the background, as talked over with Goll." One motive for discussing the setting with the playwright is that Grosz wasn't following Goll's stage rubrics. Grosz did not label his three settings by scenes. It's clear, however, that the *Ich-Du-Er* design was intended for the scene of the rendezvous between Ida and the Student (scene 5). The Odol toothpaste design (although in Goll's stage directions the advertisement for Odol is associated with the same park scene as the *Ich-Du-Er* drawings) was probably intended by Grosz to represent the Methusalem house (scene 1–4, 6, 7, 9). The Odol sign is the only bit of iconography preserved from Goll's original stage directions. A transparent window, upper right, and large blank area for projections, left third, suggest the drop suits the action at Methusalem's. The remaining scene, that of the duel (scene 8), employed a view from beneath the railing of an Eiffel-tower-like structure. Grosz mentioned the effect of a "mechanical shooting booth" in his notes. He also envisioned a transformation in the scene for the "funeral dark" by which he probably meant the exhalation of the Student's soul in the form of a winter overcoat. In the jargon of the seventies, each setting might be dubbed "high tech"; in fact they find their inspiration in the machine forms of Constructivism.

Each of these settings wrenches conventional space from its customary angle of vision as seen in normal stage settings. The walls of Methusalem's living room are cut away; areas filled with fragments of letters and signs; the window is placed too high. Conventional visual logic and order are stood on their heads. For the setting of the dueling ground the audience must discard its customary expectations, for we are asked to reconcile our normal head-on view of the stage with a perspective from beneath the scaffold structure. The white enamel letters of *Ich-Du-Er* float, creating an abstract spatial effect. References to advertising, such as the *Odol* sign, L, and signal hand in Methusalem's house, are also free-floating. The everyday object is placed in a new context which makes it fantastic. Such spatial disorientation was based on a renunciation of customary visual logic. The use of lettering, often employed in Cubist and Dada art, echoed the use of cliché in dialogue and advertisement in the play. Goll wrote prophetically of the connection between absurdity and the banality of everyday language and objects:

The absurd is today the most intellectual kind of humor and is thus the best weapon against the jargon which has dominated our lives. Ordinarily man speaks not to put his mind—but his tongue—in motion.
    . . . simultaneously the absurd will serve to illuminate the tenfold brilliance of the human brain which thinks one thing and then speaks another and then leaps and wriggles from thought to thought without the slightest sign of logical connection.[8]

At the time Grosz designed these settings, he was so enamoured of the principles of Constructivism—the embrace of the machine, of the manu-factured and popular design, of clearly defined shape and highly abstract relationship of forms—that he used a rubber stamp to sign his work, "Grosz Constr." Alexandra Exter was doing exciting Constructivist design in the USSR. Grosz visited in 1922 for six months, although it is difficult to establish if this was just before or after he completed the *Methusalem* designs. In addition, prints of Constructivist designs were available for artists of other countries who were unable to visit the USSR in person.

Grosz intended, however, to employ painted elements in conjunction with constructed three-dimensional parts. Grosz was quite specific about this in his annotations: in the case of the letters for the pronouns, *Ich Du Er*, he wrote on the drawing, "white enamelled—so called 'floating letter,' like those famous advertising letters, mounted on thin wire scaffolding." And con-cerning the iron work on the dueling ground—or above it— , he wrote, "This scaffolding should be similar to the metal railings, as in the Eiffel Tower construction, painted so it looks like metal, to be constructed meticulously."

The effect he intended to achieve was of clearly defined, two-dimen-sional forms suspended in three-dimensional space. This static setting would be modified by film and lighting effects. Behind these signs and railings there would be an abundance of color. The triangles behind the pronouns are bright orange, green, and blue. The geometric segments scattered back of the railings in the dueling ground scene are cobalt violet and blue, cool reds, violent orange, and sharp yellow-greens. The Odol setting also abounds in strong colors: a green L and a black hand float over vermillion bricks, and lemon yellow and ultramarine blue shapes.

No record exists of Grosz's reasons for changing his original—and much more conventional—costume designs. Talks with Goll may have persuaded him, or hints in Goll's stage directions about costumes, such as the Reichstag hat, or a process may have evolved out of Grosz's own work on the settings. Any or all of these connections may have brought about the change. Goll had written about masks:

The new drama must have recourse to all the technological props which are contemporary equivalents of the ancient mask. Such props are, for instance, the phonograph which masks the voice, the denatured masks, and other accoutrements which proclaim the character in a crudely typifying manner: oversized ears, white eyes, stilts. These

psychological exaggerations which we, shapers of the new drama do not consider
exaggerations, have their equivalents in the inner hyperboles of the plot . . . We seek the
most fantastic truth.[9]

Goll's notion of the mask then was directly allied to the destruction of a
particular blend of naturalistic-psychological acting, but he did not go
beyond exaggeration of human traits in his suggestion of "accoutrements
which proclaim the character in a crudely typifying manner."

Grosz's constructions extended Goll's already innovative premise. The
notion he employed was a mask for the entire figure. Instances of total
disguise exist in the history of the theatre, but rarely has the method Grosz
envisioned been employed. One account of such a production technique
exploited in a Dada performance which Goll might well have attended is the
description of Georges Ribemont Dessaigne's *L'Empereur de Chine* produced by a small theatrical laboratory, seating only 100, in Paris. Michel
Corvin describes the performance which took place in 1919 at the workshop
called "Art et Action:"

The great originality of the presentation lay in this: that the performers were reproduced
by silhouettes, made of wood and paper and which evoked the essential attributes of each
by synthetic means. It was behind or to the side of these silhouettes that the actors
played.[10]

Even the rendering of the Parisian silhouettes appears to have influenced
Grosz's practice of composing the costume constructions by means of signs
and mechanical parts, for instance: ". . . one of the two typists was reduced
to a period and a comma, the period for an eye and the comma for his
moustache." A small drawing in the lower right of his costume-construction
for Methusalem (Plate 12) shows how Grosz intended the designs to be used.
They were cutouts, basically behind which the actors moved, like men
carrying gigantic shields. Other effects, hinged members, smoke, and
perhaps even sound devices, were to have been incorporated into the
construction of the mask-shields. The fundamental form was a two-
dimensional shape propelled by an actor whose identity was—except for his
voice—concealed.

Few of us have even seen a full-length play performed entirely in
masks—much less in costumes which completely conceal the actors and
hobble their movements. What would it have been like to sit for an hour and
a half in the presence of such strange half-human marionettes? What we
normally think of as subtlety in acting, the play of gesture and expressions,
would be lost. The actor could not turn his back or move suddenly without
revealing his identity as actor. He would have to shuffle for lateral
movements.

Evaluation of such a hypothetical theatrical experience is impossible.

Several experiments and theories of masks from the early twentieth-century stage are relevant to Grosz's designs: Craig's essay on the *Über-marionette* (1907) the ballet *Parade* performed with costumes by Picasso (May 18, 1917) and the experiments in color and geometric costumes by Oskar Schlemmer for his *Triadic Ballet* (begun in 1919, planned for a production in Stuttgart in 1920, and finally performed in 1922). Whether Grosz was familiar with them, each of these events, as well as the performance of the *L'empereur de Chine*, would have been known to Iwan Goll.

In a sense Grosz's shields—with their overstatement—could be the embodiment of an interpretation by Craig's detractors of his *Über-marion-ette* theory. Craig wrote this essay in haste with little clarity, and spent much subsequent time in explaining what he did *not* mean. His goal was ensemble playing, the overthrow of the star, the removal of irritating idiosyncracies of actors which broke the unified effect he aspired to. Craig stated later that he had no intention of replacing the actor's flesh with wood or robots, exactly what Grosz's designs dared to do.

Goll's ties with *Parade* are close. He coined the German equivalent for *surréalisme*, a term which Apollinaire had invented in the original program notes of *Parade*. Goll was a member of the group about Picasso and Apollinaire. Picasso's costumes for *Parade* astonish us in part by their diversity: the manager's costumes are composed of Cubist sculpture of skyscrapers and are not stylistically related to the Chinaman's or the Acrobat's costumes. The managers' costumes, closest to the *Methusalem* designs, were unwieldy and the occupants were limited in kinds of move-ments. There are similarities, but more striking is the disparity between the set of highly unified Constructivist designs by Grosz and Picasso's more varied ones.

Oskar Schlemmer's encasements of dancers' bodies also altered move-ment. Two tacks are taken in these designs: alteration and distortion of the human body through the imposition of arbitrary geometric shape, and a less distorting description of the movement of the actor's limbs as volume. The form traced in movement was made solid, as if centrifugal motion were frozen. The latter technique appears as distortion, but represents a reality. It can be compared to the Cubist practice of simultaneous representation of different angles of vision on a single two-dimensional plane. Here simul-taneous representation of moving form was used to determine solid mass. Few of the costumes reach the maximum point of totally disguising the dancer: human heads, hands, and feet are usually there to reassure us that these are indeed men in bizarre garments.

The notion of shields to be carried by actors is an even more extreme method than Picasso's and Schlemmer's experiments, which were possible influences. The shields were consistent in design and replaced organic with machine forms, rather than attempting to arrive at a new vision of human movement. In fact, movement seems to have been a not-very-well-thought-out by-product of the visual design. Both the Schlemmer and Picasso costumes partook of the nature of sculpture. Grosz's shields were a transitional stage between painting and sculpture. They were emblematic, as the skyscraper forms of the *Parade* managers' costumes had been. The unusual devices allowed Grosz to reach his most intellectual form of satire, which is called satirical allegory in the first chapter.

Changes introduced with the new style can be most clearly traced in the metamorphoses of Ida, the Student, and the Animals. Ida becomes more of a schoolgirl and less a coquette in the Constructivist design. But on the whole, the salient elements of her costume remain constant—sash, ribbon in her hair, cross at her neck, and boots. The transposition is, in this case, almost totally stylistic. The anthropomorphic traits of the animals (who rebel in scene 2) grow stronger in the Constructivist designs: the cuckoo wears a hat and resembles a businessman, the parrot sports aviators' goggles. As the animals take on bits of human garb, the humans are depersonalized.

The Student design underwent more fundamental modification. The Constructivist version makes a more outright attack on the revolutionary's values. The illustrational Student is garbed in shaggy black, his face green, his demeanor intense, his hair long and unkempt—a comic Hamlet. His slouch is rendered geometrically in the Constructivist design. Grosz intended that smoke and noise be emitted from the head of the costume. The upper part of his head is hinged; a lighted fuse or candle is crammed between the unequal parts of visage and cranium. The yellow, black, green, lavender, and orange color scheme is typical of dissonant hues with which Grosz composed the Constructivist designs. It is doubtful that he could foresee the changing interactions of color between characters and the brightly painted scenic elements. The Student's nose is also a latch; his teeth are broken and chipped so that they resemble the piano keys of an old and out-of-tune model (Plate 14). What had been mere raggedness in the illustrational costume became a more precisely delineated, and therefore more difficult to ignore, statement in the jagged line of the Constructivist Student's cuff and coat hem. Whereas the illustrational student corresponds to a known comic type, the Constructivist design makes a sinister, if comic, statement about the incendiary values of the student.

The other costume constructions are similar assemblages of telling bits of junk, hardware, and human form rendered in geometric pattern. In the case of Veronica, the cocotte, we have two drawings for the Constructivist design, a pencil sketch and the finished watercolor. Grosz first thought of rendering his design as a side view. Veronica appears as an enormous, slightly obscene paper doll. He kept the outrageously chic hat she wears in the pencil drawing for his final version. In both Veronica and Amalia (Plate 13) Grosz rendered sexual regions with a certain explicit humor. Amalia's mouth is a perfect circle, like the aperture for a mechanical connection. Veronica's mouth is a straight, horizontal band of brilliant red. Amalia's left breast is supported by a ladder-like contraption; her abdomen resembles a great boiler. Her hat is a teapot, and other areas of her person suggest moving mechanical parts.

But the ladies are merely funny. A sort of curious gallantry existed for Grosz in his geometric assaults on the female anatomy. Methusalem (Plate 12) and his son Felix are attacked in much the manner used against the Student. Felix has legs composed of bricks, amputated arms, and the megaphone in place of a mouth which Goll's stage rubrics called for.

Methusalem raises a wine goblet in his left hand. His face is boarded over with ragged bits of wood and from the top of his head protrudes a crank-handle. Across his chest and stomach is an enormous bread knife, a double entendre for the decoration sash. His cuff links are iron crosses. A corkscrew juts from his stomach on the left. Dehumanization in these costumes allowed Grosz to assemble bits of junk and objects which symbolized the particular characteristics and values of his victim.

To see these designs as heavily influenced by Carlo Carra and Giorgio De Chirico, as Richard West does, is to underrate both their originality and the power of their satiric thrust. The slight affinity with Carra and De Chirico is less marked than similarities with Picabia's work during the same period. Use of the faceless mannequin is indeed similar. But even in a painting of the same time, such as *Republican Automatons* in the collection of the Museum of Modern Art, Grosz adopts symbols, such as the Weimar flag, the bowler, the iron cross, and letters and words, "1, 2, 3 Hurra" to satirize the bourgeois enthusiasts of the Weimar Republic. The purpose of the lack of faces in the figures is to allow Grosz to assemble, by the technique just mentioned, objects which characterize the political values of the figures. No specific value is being attacked in Carra's paintings or De Chirico's. Whereas the Carra and De Chirico paintings derive much of their strength from purposeful use of ambiguity to create mood, there is little ambiguity— spatial or thematic—in Grosz's use of dehumanized forms for satirical purposes.

Dissemination of new scenographic principles has been overwhelmingly through description in print and by graphic and photographic reproduction, rather than eyewitness observation and report. Appia's and Craig's popularity are good examples of the phenomenon in modern times; neither did many productions. However, almost every era since the invention of the printing press has followed the same pattern for distribution of scenic knowledge. Thus it mattered little, since Grosz's designs were widely reproduced, that his Constructivist shields were never used in performance. The inappropriateness of the technique to most plays is the real reason that the shield constructions have not been more widely imitated. In them, however, reside the germ for the idea for the often imitated, free-standing cutout figures Grosz used in *Schwejk*.

5

Berlin Recognizes Itself

Georg Kaiser's plays, *Kanzlist Krehler* (1922) and *Nebeneinander* (1923) portray much the same urban world as Grosz's drawings, with a similar humorous treatment of serious themes and in nearly the same stylistic ratio of Expressionism to Realism. Both artists use type characters, a device of Expressionist literature, in realistic social settings which show an inclination toward the new artistic movement of New Objectivity. The play came in a period of incredible inflation that saw the value of one dollar increase from 550 marks in July 1922 to December 1922 when the value was 7,500 marks. By August of 1923 one dollar was worth 1,000,000 marks. Grosz's drawings and Kaiser's views of the petty bourgeois world carry the same convincing quality of reportage. Critics repeatedly remarked on the inevitability of collaboration. Beyond this recognized affinity of playwright and painter for one another, whether Grosz's vision of the strata of Berlin society might have influenced Kaiser's selection of subject matter or whether the older artist might have influenced Grosz will always remain a matter for speculation. The cast of types in Grosz's portfolios, *Gott mit Uns* (1920), *Ecce Homo* (1922), and illustrated books are frequently similar to the dramatis personae of Kaiser's plays of the same period, as a comparison of Grosz's costume design for Frau Krehler with the grandmother in "God's Blessing is Visibly Upon Me" from *Gott mit Uns* shows.

These Kaiser plays, with the earlier *From Morn to Midnight*, probe the alienation and frustration of members of the lower middle class in urban society and conclude by dramatizing the impossibility of personal rebellion and independence (*Kanzlist Krehler*), as well as altruistic action (*Nebeneinander*). Both are comedies which end in suicide. Unlike the historical evasion implicit in Shaw's plays, *Caesar and Cleopatra* and *Androcles*, the sense of immediacy and contemporaneity is relentlessly pressed against the audience: throughout *Kanzlist Krehler* we see the cityscape of Berlin beyond the apartment balcony. Goll's deliberate exaggeration in *Methusalem* suggested the futility of rebellion, since men as types are bound to regenerate, duplicate their mistakes, and recommence the cycle. Beside the mask caricatures of *Methusalem* or characters from his earlier and more Expressionistic plays, Kaiser's desperately frustrated men and women might seem almost photographically reproduced. Seen in other contexts, their depiction—stripped as it is to a few primal motivations—might seem Expressionistic, and their thematic function unusually intellectualized.

Synopsis of *Kanzlist Krehler*

The events of the drama build to what appears to be a philosophical comment. Economic and social motivations apparent within the play undermine the universality of Krehler's rebellion and suicide and thus of Kaiser's comment on illusion and will power. What would seem a perfectly normal happening in the course of a routine existence, the marriage of Krehler's daughter, Ida, has the greatest effect on her father, the clerk. The play begins with the waking and breakfasting of Frau Krehler and visiting relatives on the morning after the wedding. Various doors to sleeping rooms and to the balcony across the upstage area open off the Krehlers' parlor, the play's single locale. It's now in a state of disorder—rug rolled up, dirty china and glasses about, etc.—following the ceremony. So ordinary do the petty bourgeois setting and its inhabitants seem, that we are surprised by Krehler's return from work. His first words, in Kaiser's "telegraph" style, announce the central plight of the tragicomic hero: "I—have lost—my way."[1]

His employer, Herr Rat, has sent him home on one day's leave from the office, in order to recover from the wedding festivities. Krehler is so finely attuned to his everyday schedule that the sight of open shops and crowds in the street and his new, if restricted, freedom totally disorient him. Physical bewilderment is only symptomatic of the psychological state. So relentlessly does Kaiser pursue the metaphor of disorientation that the consequences flow into philosophical implications. At first the audience may be tempted to adopt Frau Krehler's practical, comic view of the slightly ridiculous predicament of the thin, stooped old man who is so desperately estranged from his daily routine. Ida, awaking from her honeymoon night to find her father in the parlor, joins her mother in a state of astonished disbelief. Ida's considerable *joie de vivre* may contribute to Krehler's realization of what he has missed: it is she who first mentions the globe which becomes symbolic to Krehler of his deprivation and of the larger context to his existence. The first act concludes as Krehler, prodded to bed by his mothering wife, writes a note of resignation to Herr Rat.

The transformation in the parlor—from the chaotic aftermath of the party to its daily primness—marks the transition from first to second act. Krehler has been out, bought a globe, and now stands fingering it while reciting a kind of litany of places and things he might see. His wife provides a persistent antistrophe of practical questions about pension, the cost of the globe, etc. At her urging, Herr Rat arrives to dissuade Krehler from his geographical fantasies. Rat's success culminates in Krehler's destruction of the papier-mâché globe. The explosion of this world of fantasy does not, however, restore Krehler to conventional reality. Rather he turns upon his wife and daughter as causes of his exploitation. Krehler plans to let his wife starve, but she, true to type, starts looking for a job as laundress. Meanwhile the situation is solved by Max, the new husband, who returns from buying cigarettes brimming with optimism, good will, and energy. He generously offers to care for his wife's parents. All of Max's happy possibilities only embitter his antagonist, Krehler, to whom they contrast realms of discovery with his narrowing world of age and defeat.

Max and Ida's insensitivity to the desperation of her father's condition is shown in the love cooing which begins the third act. The family decides that sun and fresh air on the balcony may do Krehler good. Max is called on to adjust the awning and does so with cheerful good will. After he and Ida have retired to another room Krehler, with feigned helplessness, calls him back to readjust the shade. As Max stands on the ladder, Krehler tips it from beneath him, sending his son-in-law to certain death four stories below. When a policeman from the second floor and various bystanders assemble to inquire about the accident, Krehler, balancing precariously—but with great energy and release—demonstrates how Max swayed and fell, in the process throwing himself to the street.

1922 Production

Stifling his yawns with a sneer at a mild, uninventive season, Herbert Jhering, Berlin's most powerful critic, condescended to praise rather faintly the production of Georg Kaiser's "worst" play on February 14, 1922. The production was at the Kammerspiele of the Deutsches Theater, then managed by Felix Hollaender in Reinhardt's absence. The presentation, directed by Heinz Herald, whom we have already met as the *Dramaturg* of the puppet show, was designed by Grosz and Heartfield in one of their collaborations which was so successful that it is difficult to demarcate its boundaries. All the surviving costume sketches are by Grosz. Grosz's design for the single setting may well have been altered by Heartfield, but his name did not appear on the posters or in most of the reviews. A production photograph shows the scene as it appeared in the third act just after Max has fallen; while police and neighbors crowd in to gawk, Ida and her father are shown downstage in attitudes of surprise. Enough of the detail is visible in the production photograph to appreciate the realism of the setting with its large diamond pattern wallpaper, the glassed French doors across the balcony, and the view of the city with smokestacks and a hotel sign in the distance.

Since before the war, Kaiser's reputation had been growing steadily; *From Morn to Midnight* was receiving many productions and lots of attention. Naturally a new play attracted a considerable body of critical literature, which concentrated on the deficiencies and virtues of the play and its relationship to Kaiser's previous work. Critics found *Kanzlist Krehler* episodic, overly-intellectualized and unconvincing in its mélange of realistic and thematic details: how, they complained, could Krehler have spent 40 years at his job without a holiday? These difficulties with the play were taken into account in attempting to assess the acting style of the veteran ensemble of character players in the 1922 production.

Jhering, a director's critic, called the presentation "directorless". The judgment followed swiftly on another pronouncement condemning the management of the Reinhardt complex by Felix Hollaender. As other critics preferred to dwell on the acting and avoided the direction, Jhering may have been unpleasantly truthful. Paul Weiglin commented that the success of the production was due to the avoidance of the marionette tone in acting, an indication of Heinz Herald's and his actor's ability to root the intellectualized Kaiser characters in specificity.[2] Felix Stössinger reported that the reaction of the audience was more enthusiastic—progressing to bravos at the end of the third act—than the qualified praise of critics might indicate.[3]

Krehler was played by Paul Graetz, the cabaret singer who had brought down the house with his rendition of Mehring's and Hollaender's songs at the premiere evening of *Schall und Rauch*, three years before this Kammerspiele performance. The role of Krehler was not, however, his debut as a legitimate actor. Shortly before, he had played Tartuffe in a Kammerspiele production and several critics mentioned the improvement in his quieter and more restrained rendition of the old man. His tone varied as Krehler, and made an episodic rather than unified impression, which several critics thought Kaiser's rather than Graetz's fault. Jhering disliked his tendency to play with vehemence rather than intensity.[4] He even went so far as to suggest another actor as a substitute, a prominent figure in a production already designed by Grosz: Werner Krauss, who had played Caesar. Both men were to star in numerous silent films. The substitution, Jhering thought, would place the good performances of Krehler's antagonists, Max and Frau Krehler, in proper contrast. So talented was Graetz that it was difficult for other critics to dismiss his performance. Monty Jacobs diagnosed the source of the problem as Graetz's overexposure as a solo performer in cabarets, which made ensemble work difficult.

Remaining principal roles are rather evenly divided between Max, Ida, and Frau Krehler. Of these Ida, played by Liselotte Denera, then only 20, received the least attention from critics; one fatuous individual called her a sunbeam. Hans Brausewetter, Max, was only two years older. He had been trained in Vienna and seems to have been universally admired by the Berlin critics. Jhering noted that his performance had the rapacious vivacity of a Grosz drawing and that he was also the only member of the cast to play Kaiser's drama truly. Margarete Kupfer, who played a 60-year-old Frau Krehler, was then only about 40 herself. She was, nevertheless, an extremely experienced actress who had toured Germany in Ibsen productions, played in New York for a couple of seasons, then gone to the German provinces, and returned to Berlin in order to serve with Max Reinhardt from the early years of the century until the twenties. Jhering was annoyed with her "crowded" speech pattern, which he thought destructive to the suggestive power of the text.

Grosz's costume sketches for the Krehlers are among his least sensational and best. The general drabness appropriate to the piece is relieved only by the colored print of Frau Krehler's dress and the brightness of the old man's silk cravat. Grosz also made carefully annotated pencil drawings for the tailor at the costume shop (Plates 15 and 16). In line with Herald's realistic approach to the play, Grosz's tendency to caricature was moderated. In his costumes for Herr Rat, the Policeman, and Max he only slightly exaggerated details: a top hat for the boss, the cut of Max's knickers, the police uniform. Similarly the Grosz-Heartfield setting makes a carefully understated contrast of the gloomy parlor and the gaping view of Berlin across the Krehler balcony. Some of the elements of Grosz's original sketch are retained: the round table with a cloth in the foreground, the placement of the balcony, etc. In Grosz's sketch the drapes are wine red and the wallpaper yellow-green. In the production photograph rather careful attention to lighting, predictable from the seasoned staff at the Deutsches Theater, is visible.

In the following year, Grosz designed both sets and costumes for the next play by Georg Kaiser, *Nebeneinander*. The understatement of *Kanzlist Krehler* gave way to outspoken comment on characters and text. In five acts and fifteen scenes that necessitate six distinct locales, Kaiser developed three parallel actions which scarcely intersect. Their effect in juxtaposition is, nonetheless, powerful. *Nebeneinander* is as disturbing a play and a more satisfying one than *Kanzlist Krehler*. It is the contrasts and comparisons of the three parallel plots which suggest the suitability of the design comment Grosz made.

Synopsis of *Nebeneinander*

In the first scene, at the pawnbroker's shop, the proprietor, occasionally assisted by his daughter, deals with various customers in a rather generous manner. Among the customers is Neumann, who calls himself Niemann as he pawns a coat. While cleaning the garment, the pawnbroker discovers a letter in the pocket. Not being able to deciper the blurred address, he opens and reads the note, a farewell from one Oskar N. to Lu, a girl with whom he has had an affair. The pawnbroker is particularly alarmed to read Oskar's injunctions against the girl's possible suicide attempt. The pawnbroker resolves to set matters right by finding the author at his boarding house.

Lu, Luise, has already found refuge in the country at her brother-in-law's house. During the scene which follows the initial exposition at the pawnshop, Lu discusses the unhappy love affair with her sister. Her brother-in-law, a lock inspector, comes in with a letter.

Meanwhile the situation is viewed from a third angle as Oskar Neumann, the cad, is explaining to a friend his version of the seduction and his letter, a duplicate of which he has already mailed to Luise. The scene for this is the living room of Borsig, Neumann's future partner in a cinema enterprise.

By the end of the first act, the audience knows that the letter has been delivered, and that the lovers are alive and well, so that the following scenes in which the altruistic pawnbroker hunts for the author of the letter, thinking all the while that he may arrive too late for the unfortunate Lu, have a particularly absurd and futile quality, even pathos.

At the Pension Elvira, he meets only suspicion and an elaborate imbroglio over the identity of Neumann, alias Niemann. Meanwhile, at the lock inspector's a young man, Franz Krüger, enters the life of the recently jilted Lu. In the third scene, again at the friend of Neumann's the relationship between the host, Borsig, and Neumann becomes even closer with the entry of Borsig's sister, a would-be film star.

Following every clue, the pawnbroker decides to go to the night club (Plate 17) where, according to the letter, Lu and the by now very mysterious author of the letter first met. He makes the mistake of wearing a fur coat which has been pawned. A customer recognizes his property in the garderobe and calls the police. The pawnbroker is being hustled off to the station house for investigation in the matter of the coat as the second scene begins at the house in the country. Franz Krüger proposes to Lu, but the honest girl will not lie to the man she loves. She sends him away. In the final scene of the act, the business deal, with heavy emphasis on the financing of the movie, progresses at Borsig's.

The fourth act begins with desperate attempts by the pawnbroker to convince a sports-enthusiast police commissioner that he should use all means possible to discover the unhappy and possibly suicidal fräulein. The matter of the fur coat interests the police more. The pawnbroker is, in fact, about to lose his license for wearing the pawned article. The catastrophe which befalls the altruistic businessman is followed by a scene in which a heart-to-heart talk between Franz and Lu's sister results in explaining Lu's strange behavior to the young man. He now understands. The third plot contrasts Neumann's business success with the downfall of the pawnbroker.

The first scene of the final act is the climax of the play: as the pawnshop is officially impounded and the license revoked, the pawnbroker philosophically prepares to gas himself and his daughter. Against this grim scene is juxtaposed the happy marriage of Lu and Franz. The climber, Neumann, is no less fortunate. His success in the movie company seems a paradigm for the victories of the ruthless and selfish in a modern society.

1923 Production

The premiere performance of *Nebeneinander* November 11, 1923, was presented by a struggling and short-lived avant-garde theatre group, Die Truppe, which played in the moderate-sized Lustspielhaus. A gifted director and poet, Berthold Viertel, had begun the troupe in 1923, and their productions enlivened seasons in which the absence of Reinhardt dimmed the brilliance of Berlin theatre. Viertel wrote and acted in Viennese cabaret before working for the Austrian Volksbühne. Later he directed such films as Brecht's *Fear and Misery of the Third Reich* (1945) and eventually returned to Germany to direct for the East German Berliner Ensemble. Die Truppe's inaugural performance, heavily influenced by the Russian Tairoff's visit to Berlin, was a cubist version of the *Merchant of Venice* in which Shylock, played by Fritz Kortner, appeared to be the only realistic character moving in a carnival atmosphere of Venetian courtiers. The production, despite its ambitions, was not a success, and Jhering, the Weimar stage's pathologist, took time to write an essay[5] on the new theatre group, in which he pointed out the disparity between the ideals of *Die Truppe*; such as the abolition of the star system, stress on ensemble playing, and propagation of a literate repertoire; and the realization of these goals. Jhering suspected that the group was attempting to substitute contrived artiness for the elemental aspects of theatre.

Despite the failure of *The Merchant of Venice*, Viertel's production of *Nebeneinander* was a critical and popular success. The 1923 season had been only slightly more interesting than the year before. *Nebeneinander* was one of the few recent German plays to be performed and critical reaction was not immune from chauvinism. The play was decidedly of the moment, as the subtitle *Ein Volksstück, 1923*, indicated. The *Zeitstück* as a genre grew in popularity because of this play. Its durability can be measured by the revival at the Volksbühne in 1931. The intensity of the critics' reaction was reflected in their prose, which contained phrases, such as "Berlin recognizes itself . . . ," "Contemporaneity explodes . . . ," "the grimaces of a godless era. . . . " Reaction was not all praise. Max Hochdorf thought Kaiser was seeking success dishonestly in writing about the contemporary lives of the petty bourgeois.[6]

The cast was young and inexperienced, although talented, and this time there were no stars, like Kortner in the *Merchant*. They played as an ensemble. Kurt Aram thought the public should be eternally grateful to Viertel for proving homogeneity could still be achieved. In contrast with Herald, who had tried to make realistic all the characters of *Kanzlist Krehler*, Viertel seems to have wished to give full range to the marionette or caricatured elements of type characters. Monty Jacobs[7] noted Viertel's preference for the farcical elements of the play: the country idyll of Luise ("a folk play without folk") he rightly criticized as the weakest element of the tryptich drama. This sequence, which called for Viertel's utmost effort, was undermined by the merely adequate performances of the sisters, Luise, and the wife of the lock inspector, played by Greta Schroder and Mea Steuermann, respectively. Kaiser's pace, hobbled by the manner in which Grosz and Viertel chose to stage the play, was difficult to capture and the performance seems to have alternated between frantic playing and long waits for scene changes.

Three performers particularly attracted the critics. The qualities of Lyda Salmonova, who played the film star, seem to have been largely corporeal. As in discussion of Grosz's subjects, it is possible to speak of Kaiser types. The critics found two such incarnations among the 26 members of the cast:[8] Leonard Steckel, who played the pawnbroker, and Rudolf Forster in the role of Oskar Neumann.

Julius Bab, surveying the theatre of the Republic, speaks of Forster as one of the few old-fashioned romantic leads during the period. In the role of Neumann he turned his romanticism to caricature; "the type of opportunist." The lover became the "the cold and snazzy asphalt youth," empty-eyed, insipid, his thin lips slicing Kaiser's dialogue in precisely the correct tempo, his body forming a grotesque line. Jacobsohn still thought him too well bred for the Berlin type he portrayed.[9] Steckel, the pawnbroker, also possessed the correct Kaiser physiognomy—eyes brimming with soulfulness, muddled but inherently noble. Only in the scene at the Police Station where he protests that the police must use all possible means to find the girl and only gets himself deeper in trouble, did he become thoroughly comic. The critics were less kind to the scenery. Siegfried Jacobsohn said he would have preferred to see the play performed on a bare stage and thus avoided the 14 long pauses for construction of scenes with flats! "I would have preferred," he wrote, "to perform on a bare stage rather than putting up George Grosz' sets in fourteen atmosphere killing intermissions, although Grosz paints in an almost suffocating way what Kaiser saw: the grimace of a godless era."[10] When the curtain was lowered for set changes, the cinematic tempo which Kaiser had envisioned was broken. Clearly despite individual brilliance of certain designs, Grosz made a grave error which could only be charged to his inexperience as a designer in 1923. The distinctive format of the drama was a problem not frequently encountered in German theatre of that period; such extreme scenic demands were more likely to be found in stagings of Elizabethan plays and the first phase of Expressionism. Kaiser had apparently intended to use a stage somewhat similar to the medieval stage of polyscenic juxtaposition; in other words, with the pawnshop and secondary locales simultaneously visible. Something on this order was achieved for a later performance in 1926. Several critics pointed out that a revolve, such as they had been accustomed to seeing in Reinhardt's Shakespearean productions, would have preserved the pace.

George Kenworthy believes that cinematic techniques may have influenced Kaiser in his disposition of the stage.[11] Kenworthy also quotes Bernhard Diebold, who thought that this variety of dramatic genre and stage placement was both innovative and influential in future stagings. It's clear that a revolve or multiple revolves would have been the logical, but perhaps expensive, solution. The scenes in which the pawnbroker figures—the pawnshop, the boarding house, the police station, the nightclub—might have been staged best by placing them in center stage on a revolve. The parallel action, Neumann's rise to executive status in the movie industry and Luise's pastoral love affair, could then take place on either side or could each be mounted upon a revolve capable of turning to face upstage during the episodes in the central plot.

Despite Grosz's technical miscalculations, his individual settings are among his most interesting and display his power in effectively deploying a few symbols. The designs are organized with a series of vertical planes parallel to the footlights. The designs were executed so that this quality of painting remains in the finished product. In the setting for the police station an enormous red gibbet looms over a dark grey courtyard with barred windows. A corner office area is set up at half-height center stage, with the vertex of two walls at the center line. A low balustrade parallel to the footlights divides the area within the walls from the general stage area. Stage left an enormous paragraph sign, Grosz's persistent reference to Weimar's outdated legal codes, symbolizes the place, as do the stripes of the Weimar flag painted within the office and the outsize handcuffs dangling from a stand-up desk on the stage right side. In the center beneath the gibbet is a large eagle affixed to the low balustrade; it has the impact of later Nazi propaganda displays. In the settings for Borsig's room and the nightclub Grosz parodies the pretensions of modern interior decoration. Simpler than the powerful police station, they are basically flats with allusions to architectural detail. Most of the settings employ some form of sign: the cubist pin-up in Borsig's room, the pawnbroker's sign in his shop, the eagle and paragraph in the police station, the numbered doors in the hallway of the Pension Elvira (Plate 18), and the men's room sign in the nightclub (Plate 17). Grosz was coming close to stripping away all superfluities in realism and enlarging signs and symbols as instant—almost telegraphic—

indications of locale. In the lock inspector's house in the country, Grosz employed four flats grouped to form a three-sided room with an exterior door and a fourth flat added to the stage right side which contains a door, facing head-on to the audience, leading to the rest of the small house. Treetops and a picket fence indicate the rural landscape beyond. Within the play there is a strange battle between elements of Naturalism or New Realism and caricature, and the same tension permeates Grosz's designs for both sets and costumes. The sight of real properties—the heavy armchairs in Borsig's room, the gramophone—placed against the stylized architectural details is somewhat incongruous. The enormous cycloramic effect of windows at night in the courtyard of the police station, which was also partially visible backing the nightclub scene, serves beautifully the combination of realism and artificially exaggerated statement that Kaiser used. Caspar Neher used a similar effect in his designs for Brecht's *Trommeln in der Nacht* in 1922 one year before the *Nebeneinander* production. The integration of interior and exterior cityscape was to become almost a "type" setting in following years. Several critics saw Grosz's powerful use of color and symbol as caricaturing the play; one critic spoke of Grosz's "distorting mirror" style, which expressed the character that dominates each scene while ignoring the conventional reality.[12]

Some of Grosz's costumes are highly realistic. The design for the wife of the lock inspector is one of these which comes closest to realism. But the false chic of the movie starlet is caricatured to the point of grotesqueness in Grosz's design for a costume which Lyda Salmonova never actually wore (Plate 19), as the production photo from Borsig's room shows.

The tension between various production elements is not due simply to muddle-headedness on the part of the creators. Great—perhaps too great—demands are made on the audience. In *Nebeneinander* they were asked to see themselves not in photographic realism, but from a number of angles. Expressionistic elements commented upon realistic aspects of production. The creators were not aiming at a unified emotional and intellectual experience; they avoided the hypnosis induced by realism. In embryo this tension and cross-commentary relates to the "epic" staging which Piscator was about to develop and which forms the core of Brecht's distinctive manner of staging his own plays and adaptations.

6

Collaboration with Piscator

Erwin Piscator offered his old friend George Grosz the opportunity to participate in important collective creations. Prior to his professional association with Piscator in 1926, Grosz had worked with relatively "weak" directors who could neither fully use nor dominate his talents.

Grosz was not, like Craig, a director-designer whose designs embodied a single principle which could be used to determine acting style, tempo, and characterization. The closest he had come to such an overall concept was in *Methusalem*, and the credit for these designs must certainly be shared with Iwan Goll. As a political satirist Grosz had trained himself to stand aside, to observe, and to comment upon events and people. This training could not be willfully dropped in the theatre, so that, partially, his approach had always to be a "gloss" or critical comment on the events and characters of the production.

Piscator's method of directing—a free collaboration in which designer, technical director, and authors were, at least ideally, members of a collective—suited Grosz. Piscator instinctively resented the bourgeois myth of the artist as a lonely, tormented individual struggling with a separate fate. Like Brecht, Piscator genuinely believed in collaborative creation, even though, also like Brecht, he could not always restrain his own egotism and superior powers.

The friendship which had preceded the collaboration perhaps eased the potential conflict between director and designer. Wieland Herzfelde introduced Grosz to Piscator. From Berlin, Grosz wrote asking for tea while Piscator was at the Ypes front in 1917. The joking request was complied with:

> I sent some tea to George Grosz. And this little tea parcel started a friendship that lasted until death. We did not only have tea, or even tea with . . . We got intoxicated on all kinds of beverages. We intoxicated each other with wine, wine spirits, the spirit in the wine, the wine in the spirit, the spirit in general, the dialectics, dadaism, photo collages, sketches for scene designs, politics . . .[1]

Such shared experiences and beliefs were perhaps less important to the works they created than their similar reactions to World War I; in particular, they had both suffered in field hospitals. Equal contempt for the art of the past animated both artists in the years following the war, the Dada period. Piscator was full of admiration for Grosz because the draftsman was the only member of the Dada circle to make a name for himself, to menace the Establishment. Piscator admired Grosz's contradictory nature: "He was a great artist of our time. And an even greater man."[2]

In the early twenties, Grosz and Piscator traveled parallel routes to notoriety, with Piscator progressing at a slightly slower pace. His earliest theatre was *Das Tribunal* (1919–1920) in Königsberg. Then he moved to the Proletarisches Theater in Berlin (1920–21); next to the Central-Theater before the Rotters took over (1923–24); and finally to the Volksbühne am Bülowplatz (1924–27), where among continual turmoil he did his finest work. Two of these theatres, the Proletarisches and the Central, were attempts to establish theatres in the form which Piscator thought the already long-existing Volksbühne ought to assume. In 1927 he was forced out of the Volksbühne and formed his own Theater am Nollendorfplatz. The tenets of the founders of the Volksbühne, to bring art to the culturally deprived, no longer sufficed for Piscator. A new Volksbühne must foster a program of political awareness. Directors and critics, such as Julius Bab, had seen in the Volksbühne productions a hypothetical meeting ground in which the tensions of class warfare were to be relaxed and diverted to Art. But Piscator insisted that a proletarian audience had the right to be proletarian, that they should not have to adopt the manners and hushed respect of the middle classes for the concept of culture. Why should they check their reactions as an egocentric actor postured before them delivering a text which had only the most distant relationship to their time and lives? Theatre was meant to be enjoyed, much as a boxing match at the local sports arena. Theatre was political progaganda; the audience must be informed. It must also participate. Perhaps from his Protestant clergymen forefathers, Piscator inherited a strong desire to preach. He virtually rewrote productions in order to do this. Epilogues and prologues were affixed, sometimes filmed, and a great deal of the information therein seemed beside the point to reviewers who resented the condescension implicit in Piscator's informing. One critic congratulated the director on his forebearance in omitting a history of Prague, from its founding to the war, as a documentary prologue to *Schwejk*. Piscator's audience, the 140,000 subscribers to the Volksbühne, was by no means proletarian in toto; some young workers came to Piscator productions and stood to sing the Internationale at the finale, but the major source of excitement and critical controversy came from Liberals and déclassé intellectuals. The professional classes who had only their services to sell, doctors, lawyers, etc., also yielded audiences desiring a political theatre. Prices were high: 16 marks for an orchestra seat in the Piscator Bühne at the Nollendorfplatz theatre. To homogenize his audience Piscator seated subscribers throughout the theatre. Piscator and his theatres supplied an inexhaustible source of political and economic contradictions for his critics. Piscator describes the "birth of epic theater" when Heartfield arrived late for a performance of *The Cripple* with a backdrop he had just painted; the scene is better if you remember that Heartfield was small:

> What then happened might have looked like a director's gimmick, yet it just happened. Heartfield: "Stop, Erwin, stop! I'm here." . . . "We waited almost half an hour for you (murmur of agreement from the audience) and then we had to start without your backdrop." Heartfield: "You didn't send the car! It's your fault! I ran through the streets, the streetcars wouldn't take me because the cloth was too big" . . . And since he refused to calm down I turned to the audience and asked them what was to be done, should we continue to play, or should we hang up the backdrop? There was an overwhelming majority for the backdrop. . . . (Nowadays I refer to John Heartfield as the founder of the "Epic Theater.")[3]

The Political Aesthetic had to be implemented with new techniques. *New* should be qualified, for they were frequently borrowed from the "decadent" revue form. Piscator's work on the *Revue Roter Rummel* (1924) proved a discovery ground for the recasting of decadent bourgeois forms into functional propagandist techniques. The discarding of conventional dramatic structure, the ignoring of unity of action, and the exploitation of presentational entertainment were modes which could be effectively transferred to the new theatre. Heartfield designed for Piscator when he made his first efforts for the propaganda section of the Communist Party. Considering his association with Heartfield and Grosz, one is not surprised that Piscator was among the first to exploit the techniques of photomontage, developed by Grosz and Heartfield during their Dada period, on stage. Heartfield designed the revue, *Trotz alledem*, at the Grosses Schauspielhaus using a practical platform and film projections.

Particularly in the early productions Piscator adopted the stance of the opponent of taste, the antagonist of Bourgeois Art. Sweeping aside the tasteful concerns of Max Reinhardt, for instance, he quickly reduced the stage to a few essential levels, properties, and films which were frequently taken from newsreels rather than specially shot for the performance. Jessner had also eliminated the picturesque and charming from his productions, substituting for painted scenery the super-bare stagings of the Staatstheater; but he had replaced the clutter of scenery, left over from the bourgeois theatre, with platforms of an extreme severity, reflecting a contrived and consummately "tasteful" restraint. To his credit, Piscator was a more ruthless modernist or a more genuine philistine than his colleague, a captive of the Establishment, who nevertheless defended Piscator when controversial productions at the Volksbühne divided subscribers into factions.

Chief among Piscator's problems was finding scripts which conformed

with his political aesthetic. Existing classics rarely made the direct statements and embodied the Marxist principles of history which he wanted to
drive home to his audiences. Increasingly he turned to nondramatic material,
particularly to adaptations of novels. Frequently he urged the writers of the
Left, such as Toller and Mehring, to write for his stage. Occasionally, he
committed the error of updating classics in a desperate attempt to make
them relevant to modern audiences. Fortunately the three plays which which
Grosz was concerned were contemporary creations. They represent the
strongest innovations, and the vein which would provide the greatest yield
for new productions: ideas, techniques, and comic sensibilities.

The Political Aesthetic and its by-products were riddled with contradictions which mattered very much to critics at the time and less and less as
the perspective of history reduced these productions to their broad outlines.
Piscator was criticized from the Left for not finding new revolutionary plays;
from the Right for radicalizing already existing works. Fundamental to the
paradoxes of Piscator's theatre was the attempt of the new Political Theater
to exist within the old economics of the capitalist society. Needs were even
more basic than finding a supportive audience: Gropius designed an ideal
theatre seating 4,000, in which space for elaborate machinery was combined
with audience space, which would allow exploitation of a "hit." The
economic feasibility of a program such as Piscator's was to be the final
breaking point in the Political Aesthetic. In order to present the best
productions, Piscator wished to use "stars," such as Tilla Durieux and Max
Pallenberg; most of his actors, on the other hand, were young, unknown,
and without the formidable presence needed to perform with actors who
overbalanced them in talent, experience, and prestige. Critics pointed out
that Piscator's theatrical workers were paid substandard wages; that participation in the star system was a concession to current economics; and that
the stars, particularly Durieux, had to finance the productions for him. His
school and "studio" seem not to have functioned well during their relatively
brief existence. Piscator was as vulnerable from the Left as Right, and far
more responsive. Brecht rewrote *Boom* in order to please the Communist
Party, thus displeasing the star and adding reversals which cast the entire
evening into a muddle.

Toller's *Wandlung*

The first production which Grosz designed for Piscator was not presented.
These designs for a proposed staging of Toller's *Wandlung* are the only area
of Grosz's theatrical career which has remained totally unexplored: until
recently the sketches were hidden in the estate collection. Plans were begun
in 1926 while Piscator was at the Volksbühne am Bülowplatz. Our only hint

of Piscator's interest in the play comes from a passage in *Das politische Theater* in which he discusses his desire to stage the great success of early Expressionist drama in a more radical and, to him, more realistic manner than the first performance, directed by Karl Heinz Martin:

> When in the winter of 19/20, I opened my own theater in Königsberg which was, significantly enough, called The Tribunal, I planned a production of *Wandlung* which was to differ in principle from the Berlin production in that the settings were to be constructed as realistically as possible (the reality of the war as I had actually experienced it). I even reworked the language in order to suggest to Toller (may he forgive me, the blackness of this thought is unknown to him to this day!) how he might free his style of its lyrical Expressionism. The Expressionist school provided no pointer for me. I was already too deeply committed politically.[4]

Rather typically, the play did not suit Piscator, who was rarely satisfied with anyone else's dramatic efforts. He was probably correct in thinking that the poetic language of Toller was not the proper manner in which to develop a hard-hitting, antimilitaristic thesis. Piscator admired the attempt to cope with contemporaneity, but not the terms in which the effort was carried on. The *O-Mensch*, humanitarian revolution was too vague and too individual a message for Piscator. The play dealt with war in terms of the revolt of an individual rather than in the perspective of a collective fate. It made the war a conflict of men rather than the negation of humanity by machines. *Wandlung* was a great popular success of Expressionist drama, but in its sprawling lyric scope, it is as outdated today as Piscator predicted that it would be:

> This drama was, of course, also a "revolution" but a revolution of individualism. Man, the individual rebelled against Fate. He appeals to his fellows, as "brothers". He wants the love of all men for all men, humility of every man towards every other. This drama is lyrical, i.e. undramatic. These are dramatized lyrical poems. In the misery of war, a war which in reality had been a war of machines against men, they sought a way through negation toward the "soul" of many. So these dramas were deeply reactionary, a reaction against the war, but against the collectivism of war too, a reaction in favor of a newly found concept of ego and of certain elements in prewar culture. . . . It was a mixture of personal experience (lyrical) destiny (dramatic), politics (epic). The predominance of the "poet" in Toller, who formulated not facts but judgments, evaluations ethical abstractions and these "poetically" explains why it became neither a clarion call nor a contemporary play which transcended its own time, nor an "eternal value" in the sense of pure art.[5]

Considering this rather extreme case of ambivalence toward the play, it is curious that Piscator considered the drama for *Das Tribunal* and even more interesting that he came so close to presenting it at the Volksbühne. He can only have planned to radicalize it and to prune some of its lyricism. Clearly, Grosz's settings were intended to bolster the realism, to provide an arsenal for attack when Toller's outrage faltered or became too highly individualized. Grosz was torn between Expressionism, in a violent manner, and tight realism, along the lines of his entry into the New Realism period.

Synopsis of *Wandlung*

The 14 scenes of *Wandlung* are held together almost solely by the appearance in each episode of Friedrich or his double, the representative of his subconscious, a man with Friedrich's features. About half of the scenes are designated by Toller as "realistic"; in these Friedrich deals with actual happenings. In the "dream" scenes, which frequently anticipate the subsequent events in "real" scenes, Friedrich's double undergoes a variety of metamorphoses. The transformation or transfiguration of the title refers to Friedrich's change from militant patriot to humanist-revolutionist. The shadow of *A Dream Play* envelops Toller's first dramatic effort; the supposedly realistic scenes are hardly that, if only because of the inflation of the language. The six stations form a curious division, obscurely honoring Strindberg; Piscator and Grosz felt no compunction in planning an evening which divided the text into the conventional three-act format.

In the Prologue, Death-by-Peace, an allegorical figure, confronts Death-by-War, garbed in an army helmet, over rows of graves (Plate 20). Death-by-Peace eventually rejects the hegemony of Death-by-War.

Having set the stage with an unrealistic scene, Toller turned to a battle which is a staple in the bourgeois myth of the artist. The aspiring sculptor, Friedrich, argues with his bourgeois mother in a town house at the Christmas season(First Sta., i, Plate 21). Friedrich is torn between his identification with the Wandering Jew and attempts to integrate in German society. When a friend enters to announce the outbreak of war, Friedrich seizes the opportunity to prove his patriotism, to rebel against his family, and to belong to the world of love he sees in the Christians' Christmas lights decorating the city streets. It is characteristic of the scenes that they follow abruptly and without logical transition. The "dream" action aboard a troop train (Sta. I, ii,) portrays the disillusionment of soldiers with the war, long before Friedrich undergoes similar experiences. Friedrich's double and another figure, with a skull in place of his head, sit listening to several soldiers discuss their endless suffering. The planes are reshuffled as we switch to a "realistic" action (St. II, iii), in which Friedrich argues for patriotism with a group of soldiers who deny his equal citizenship because he is a Jew. At the conclusion of the scene Friedrich proves himself by volunteering for a dangerous patrol. Mechanically, too symmetrically, we return to the hallucinated actions: skeletons leave their entrapment in barbed wire to dance about the skeleton of a girl who has been raped by troops. Next, the outcome of Friedrich's patrol is portrayed in the field hospital (Sta. III, v) where he is brought, in delirium, badly treated at first until the arrival of a colonel who decorates him for his bravery. Perhaps the most grotesque scene, one in the hallucinated manner, repeats the hospital setting (Sta. III, vi). A group of amputees is made to parade before visiting doctors. Friedrich's double, a medical student, faints. He reenters the action as a priest, but confronted with the pain of the patients, he breaks his crucifix at their reproaches. A more "realistic" scene is Friedrich's studio, where he is at work on a monument to the Fatherland (Sta. IV, vii). As he works, he is interrupted by several visitors. First comes his friend, then the sister of the friend, Gabriele, Friedrich's beloved. She breaks off with the young sculptor. To this disillusionment are added the visits of a syphilitic woman and her even more severely afflicted husband, who turns out to be a former army comrade of Friedrich's. His revulsion from patriotism seems complete, for he attempts to destroy the monument on which he is working, then to shoot himself. His sister comes to dissuade him, offering him an alternative to suicide in the mystical realization of his own humanity.

The path of discovery is first depicted in a scene in which Friedrich's double is lodging with a wretchedly poor woman and her daughter to whom he makes love (Sta. V, viii). He is led by a night visitor to a factory. Friedrich disappears in these scenes, and we meet only the adventures of his double; the seesaw action of alternate dream and real scenes is broken, as three scenes of the double follow without break. The factory to which Friedrich's double has been brought turns out to be a prison, as he first thought. He is a prisoner (Sta. V, ix) about to be tried for murder. He dies, after a woman, pregnant with his child, rushes in; the other prisoners form a circle about the newly-born child and mother at the conclusion of the scene. Once more (sc. x) Friedrich's double is heard declaring a new awakening as he moves along a country road. In a meeting hall (sc. xi) Friedrich preaches love in the maw of hunger, with little success. Next (Sta. VI, sc. xii) two climbers move across a rockface: Friedrich's double and his friend's. Friedrich's abandons the friend's.

The final scene, the end of Friedrich's spiritual wandering, takes place in a square before the village church (xiii). Friedrich encounters his mother, who refuses to be reconciled with her son. An uncle treats him similarly. The doctor from the field hospital turns up, once more babbling idiotically of panacea in a water cure. A sick man can offer no solution to the riddles of life and society but the building of public lavatories and suicide. Friedrich's only sympathetic encounter is with his sister, whom he tells of his approach to humanity. The play concludes as Friedrich exhorts a crowd to revolution built upon the realization of its own humanity. The crowd responds to Friedrich:

> Brothers, stretch out your tortured hands
> With cries of radiant, ringing joy!

Stride freely through our liberated land
With cries of Revolution, Revolution![6]

Proposed Staging

Remembering the unfavorable comments on his *Nebeneinander* designs, and taking advantage of the abundant technical resources of the Volksbühne theatre, Grosz set these 14 complicated scenes on a revolving stage. Working with thin strips of paper and pencil notations, he made a collage in which platforms and backdrops were positioned on the revolve, a permanent feature of the stage, over 19 meters in diameter. The portal opening of the stage was only about 16 meters. Later he made ground plans which indicated the changing of scenes.

These are the only Grosz ground plans extant, to my knowledge, but they show him considering the production from its practical vantage and demonstrate his deeper immersion in the craft of scene design.

The ground plans show that Grosz intended to construct, rather than to project, elements of the dream or hallucinated sequences. Bold, Expressionist brush drawings might, at first glance, indicate otherwise, for they appear to call for rendering as projections. Ground plans contradict the impression first made by the ink drawings, as do the more careful watercolor and pencil sketches. That these designs are studies and that Grosz and Piscator never reached the stage of finished production plans should not diminish interest in the drawings and tentative proposals.

Piscator, as already quoted, wished to make the production more realistic. The way to do this was clearly not by following Neppach's Expressionist designs, effective as they seem in photographs used in the 1919 *Wandlung* premiere. The tendency toward realistic setting—in fact, this is one of the most realistic settings of Grosz's career—is shown in his most finished sketch, the watercolor for the first scene of the first station. In the foreground, a wagon carries a miniature box set, walls cut away in jagged lines, which is Friedrich's family's house. In another study of the same setting, the wagon carrying the room is more centrally positioned and the proportions are better: the room is larger in relation to the surrounding city streets. As in several of the *Nebeneinander* settings, the city envelops the house. Grosz labored at the perspective of a row of shops in the background. Fastidious attention to architectural details and to lighting effects, particularly in the relationship of a string of Christmas lights to the night sky, is apparent. The stage left section of a building, with its enormous girders, suggests a vastly simplified design, in contrast to the rather fussy details on the drop to the opposite side.

Grosz seems hamstrung in these designs, not by the realism but by the necessity of using conventional techniques of scenography: the ground row, painted drop, and wagons. That he was thinking, and hampered in his thinking, in these terms is demonstrated by his designs for the second scene of the First Station. This sketch shows that he intended to continue the realistic vein even in one of the "hallucinated" scenes. Stage right an open car stands; stage left the rubble of a destroyed church coheres. All the elements are shown parallel to the footlights, as if Grosz constantly were anxious about the physical execution of his setting and so employed conventional painted scenery which, because of its familiarity, he could control.

The vague idealism of the play might well have profited from Grosz's realistic approach in these settings. Had *Wandlung* been realized in this manner it would certainly have been a departure from the nonrepresentational structures, similar to those of Meyerhold which Piscator was using in the early years at the Volksbühne. Grosz did not take up the realistic vein again until he designed *Der Kandidat* and *Grischa*. The Expressionist drawings may have had some influence on the projections for *Schwejk*. There are, indeed, a group of drawings which seem equally appropriate to either production. The Piscator version of *Schwejk* was as polemical as *Wandlung*, and in certain moments, as in the suggested parade of cripples at the end, directly recalled scenes and images of *Wandlung*.

Zech's *Das trunkene Schiff*

In the months following the proposals for *Wandlung*, Piscator actually presented a play designed by Grosz, *Das trunkene Schiff* by Paul Zech, a drama less overtly political than *Wandlung*, but more revolutionary in techniques of staging. Zech, a poet, translator, and biographer of Rimbaud, was even more concerned with the plight of individual genius than Ernst Toller. The protagonist of his play, Rimbaud, offered considerably more interesting adventures than Toller's semiautobiographical Friedrich. The play is an accurate biographical piece embroidered with imaginative glimpses through keyholes. The frank treatment of homosexuality in the Verlaine-Rimbaud relationship shocked some reviewers. The form owed much to the loose construction of Expressionist plays; the subtitle, aptly enough, was "eine szenische Ballade." Predictably, Piscator was disappointed in Zech's failure to reintegrate his hero into the political events of his time:

> In Paul Zech's work, too, there were points at which he was beginning to come to grips with the stuff of the times (the War of 1870, the Paris Commune, the Third Republic in France, the whole transitional period of French history from which a figure like Rimbaud is inseparable). But he, too, unfortunately never got beyond individual psychology and even there he could not see the Anarchism of the individual clearly enough for the good of the play; here again the dramatist transfers his own lyrical feelings, and projects them on his fellow poet Rimbaud.[7]

There is every evidence that throughout the production Piscator tried to minimize the psychological speculation. Also, one of the functions of Grosz's projected drawings was to provide references to social and political events. Grosz's projections were not usurping the place of conventional scenery; there had been very little of that on Piscator's stage, but they were fulfilling the function of specifying the locale of a particular scene. An extremely sophisticated use of slides to unfold the narrative of Rimbaud's travels, with elision of time and space within a single projection, was employed. An enormous amount of technical information was also gathered in the course of the production, making possible the successful animated film effects in *Schwejk.*

Piscator at first considered a revolving three-sided screen, a revival of the Greek, and then Renaissance, *periaktoi* device. He eventually discarded this format for a triptych screen. The side panels could be folded forward or backward independently. With both sides in forward position the screen formed a room-like enclosure. Platforms, set pieces, and furniture were placed in front of the screens. Piscator described the modification of his initial idea:

> In order to help these fast flowing vignettes of an extraordinary life achieve a fast dramatic pace, we intended to erect a screen on a small revolving disc, onto which projectors that were on the large revolve, would project a scenic illustration. The actor would have been moved onto the stage by means of the revolve; all scenic movement was, therefore, supposed to happen without interruption. All the machinery should animate itself before the audience. This idea—that could be used in staging a number of modern plays, especially those by Brecht, Paquet, Kaiser and Toller—could not be executed for technical reasons, and still has to be tried out in a later production.[8]

Piscator's use of the triptych screen, it should be noted, occurred in the same year as Abel Gance's use of a similar three-part screen for his epic film, *Napoleon.* Piscator's production came months before, but there are also overlapping interests in the use of film montage.

Synopsis of *Das trunkene Schiff*

The action sprawls over two continents and a time span of 23 years, from Rimbaud's departure from the family farm at the age of 17 to his death in 1891. There are 17 distinct settings. The first, a garden beside a river bank, is the provincial landscape from which Rimbaud flees. The adolescent, both dreamy and prankish, confides in an old farmer. While a village girl distracts the old man, Rimbaud steals away. The next scene, in the railroad switchyard, contrasts with the bucolic tranquility of the first setting. Strolch, a tramp, steals Rimbaud's watch and closes the door of the box car before the boy can jump in. The young vagabond is taken into custody by the railyard police. Meanwhile in Paris (sc. ii) Verlaine, his wife Mathilde, and several distinguished literary gentlemen await the arrival of the prodigy whose poems they have read. A nervous and irritable Verlaine disbelievingly reads passages of *Le Bateau ivre*, comparing them to classic works of genius. Mathilde and the maid are disturbed over the "wedding feast" Verlaine has ordered for the arrival of the unfamiliar poèt. The maid does not at first wish to admit the young, muddy vagabond who knocks. Mathilde, shocked at his age, regains her composure sufficiently to make him welcome.

Very early in the morning, within a public park, Verlaine and Rimbaud disport (sc. iii). Verlaine's protegé wears new clothes. Verlaine hints at his passion, Rimbaud at his distaste for Mme. Verlaine. Narrowly avoiding arrest by a park policeman, they decide to return to chez Verlaine for breakfast. Rimbaud's corruption of his friend, particularly his effect on the marriage, is impressionistically explored in the following scenes. The conversation revolves around Rimbaud's pernicious influence as the literati sit about a small table in a Latin Quarter Cafe (Plate 22). Anatole France counsels reason: Rimbaud insults the novelist. Rimbaud is already fed up with Paris, wanting now to escape to the North. Above all he cannot abide the domestic situation in the Verlaine ménage. He constantly threatens Verlaine with imminent departure.

In a garret (Plate 23) Anatole confirms Mme. Verlaine's worst suspicions. Rimbaud enters, resentful at Mathilde's and Anatole's intrusion; then Verlaine comes in for a final demonstration of his helplessness before Rimbaud's willful manipulation. Next, the two friends have left Paris as they planned in the scene before (sc. vi). Rimbaud is disgusted by Verlaine's chasing of country girls; he aspires to be off adventuring. And Verlaine attributes Rimbaud's malaise to his no longer writing. In Brussels (sc. viii) Rimbaud and Verlaine have returned from England and joined Mathilde at a café. Rimbaud believes he is about to leave from Antwerp on his adventures, but Verlaine and his wife plan to return the adolescent to his mother in Charleville. Rimbaud completely rejects Verlaine, but more especially the bourgeois life Verlaine is returning to in Paris. Mathilde's plans to make him a clerk in a few years, so that he can be in Paris, are the ultimate humiliation. As Rimbaud gets up to go to Antwerp to meet his ship, Verlaine draws a pistol, fires, and wounds Rimbaud.

In his solitary prison cell at Mons (sc. viii, Plate 24) where he has been confined following the attempted murder, Verlaine is visited by a priest. Although he will be released in a week, Verlaine's alternatives for the future seem forfeit: Mme. Verlaine is remarried, Rimbaud sends an unforgiving message from Stuttgart where he has become tutor to a rich family, and the priest wants Verlaine to join a religious order.

His course turns out to be pursuing Rimbaud. Beside a lake, Rimbaud, dressed in newly acquired clothes, walks and quarrels with a girl (sc. ix). As the girl runs away when Rimbaud pessimistically denies his love, Verlaine, who has been following them, approaches. Verlaine's only desire is to be with Rimbaud; Rimbaud's only desire is to be free of Europe and all entanglements.

Abruptly, the scene is Cyprus (Plate 25, sc. x) where gangs of Negro slaves crush rocks under a blazing sun and the watchful eyes of their white keepers. With his faithful servant, Hassan, Rimbaud analyzes the situation: exploitation, and potential revolt. He is the first agitator against the colonialist slave labor; as the scene closes the workers carry him about on their shoulders.

On the terrace of a trading post in Aden, Rimbaud drinks with the trader, Labatut (sc. xi). As they drink Rimbaud bargains with the colonial on behalf of his workers. He brags of his newly acquired wealth, and in a delicate maneuver Rimbaud extracts himself by calling attention to a black princess, an offering to the colonial.

At a tent camp farther in the interior (sc. xii), Rimbaud examines his discolored teeth. Despite the urgings of his servant, Hassan, Rimbaud is intoxicated by the accumulation of wealth, even to the point of destruction of his physical being. The conflict between dependence and independence is duplicated in his relationship with Hassan; he screams for firewood, but rejects Hassan's efforts to ease the pain.

Rimbaud's disloyalty to his own identity as a European is thrown up to him by a missionary in the following scene (xiii). Simeon tries to upbraid Rimbaud with past relationships: Verlaine, his family, and his European heritage. Limah, a native mistress, occupies Rimbaud's thoughts, but he yields his place beside her in the leaf hut to Hassan at the close of the scene. In one more African episode, on the eve of a great battle Rimbaud confronts the colonialist Tschillay, completes the story of his rejection of Europe, and attempts to live in a primitive culture (sc. xiv).

Rimbaud, racked with fever and gangrene, abandons Africa on board the *Pinguin* (sc. xv). He is stretched out on an improvised bed and cared for by a young sailor as a stormy sea exacerbates his hallucinations and self-pity.

Miraculously he survives the trip and the next scene returns to his native village (sc. xvi, Plate 26). The old farmer with whom Rimbaud spoke in the prologue now discusses the cripple who has returned from his African adventures. The old man speaks to an offstage voice, and not until the end of the scene do we learn that it is that of Rimbaud's mother.

The final scene is entitled "Haven" and portrays Rimbaud's death in the hospital in Marseille. He alternates between hallucinations of his voyages and repentance, desires to be a solid, middle class citizen. The priest comes, but it is his sister, rather than the nurse, doctor, or priest, who comforts him. The attendant, a personification of death, comes for the body before Rimbaud has succumbed, and this final effect is one of the strongest moments—and one of the few dramatic ones—in the play.

In writing of his production, Piscator was forced to give a brief synopsis outlining the action, and it is interesting to note that he minimizes the psychological bent of the play:

> At the age of seventeen, the phenomenal genius Arthur Rimbaud visits Verlaine who introduces him to the intellectual world of Paris. The older more sensitive poet developed an inescapable dependency on the stronger Rimbaud. The friendship of these two great Bohemians came to a violent breakup caused by Rimbaud's disgust with the literature, the decadent, mendacious culture of Europe and its intellectual representatives. He turns his back on literature and Europe and becomes a colonist of self-discovered African lands. He befriends the Africans, becomes their first agitator and leads a life filled with work and adventures which is put to an early, painful end in a Marseille hospital.[9]

The Projections

Grosz's drawings for *Das trunkene Schiff* are the most lyric he made for the theatre, even anticipating his preoccupation with the natural arabesques of the landscape in his American period. Grosz customarily employed a fine brush line in black ink; the majority of the drawings are patterned so that the overall effect resembles a textile design; most of the ink drawings were subsequently enlivened with washes of transparent watercolor. The color is vivid, on the whole unrealistic and emotional, and occasionally, as in the study for the farmyard (Plate 26), too saccharine to be truly pleasing.

Grosz's working process with Piscator can be demonstrated by comparing a first study for the Paris café (Plate 22) in the collection of the Museum of Modern Art and a production photo of the same scene.

From the production photo we know that there were modifications in the composition of the drawing. Enough of the original content and form were kept, however, to make the kinship of the drawing and photograph apparent. Piscator exercised an editorial veto power and asked for changes in the early sketches. Those chosen by Piscator were finished by Grosz and photographed by I. A. Hübler-Kahla of the Volksbühne for use as projections.

The projections functioned in a number of remarkable ways which should be outlined here, and in some cases treated in detail in more specific discussion of the individual drawings. They were intentionally picturesque, providing "local color" necessary to Rimbaud's imaginary and real voyages. Needless to say, this kind of guide indicating locale to the audience could not be provided by the constructions frequently employed by Piscator or by the super-bare platforms and steps in favor with Jessner. Equally difficult would have been the construction of so much realistic scenery. Max Reinhardt had once astounded audiences by placing a "real" forest with "real" moss before them. Imagine, however, the difficulties in duplicating African vegetation on stage. A viable alternative was found in projected scenery. The scenery made no attempt to compete with the reality of the actors. It was not simply the signboard which some scholars have thought facilitated Elizabethan staging and which was to be used by Brecht. The projections had their own visionary identity: a role midway between illusion and information. In order to place the actor and the projection on the same level of reality in certain scenes, Piscator moved his players behind the screen so that they cast silhouettes. For the Cafe in Aden he positioned the native princess behind the screen: "The silhouettes behind the center screen suggest the street scene in front of the cafe, without abandoning the principle of drawing and without ever being practically installed on stage."[10] Sometimes a very subtle magic trick was performed, probably without the audience's conscious knowledge: time and space were elided. The locales of events which were to happen sequentially were presented simultaneously. A double function existed in the lighting; Grosz could present dramatic lighting effects in his watercolors, such as the contrast between a darkened interior and skylight, the blazing sun, explosions and moonlight, in the projections. The lighting of the foreground of the stage area remained constantly rather dark—so that the actors were always "in the theatre." This was a remarkable way of presenting emotionally charged lighting effects while maintaining distance and even antiillusionism.

Flexibility was the keynote. The projection method permitted Piscator to use realistic set pieces and occasionally, as in the setting for Rimbaud's voyage on the *Pinguin*, film projections. Motion pictures of waves surged on the screen behind co-designer Edward Suhr's realistically designed set piece representing the ship deck and mast. This kind of effect was pure illusionism.

The potentially disruptive effects of caricature were much less an issue in this production, for the projections were usually landscapes. There are three exceptions in which caricature, or as one critic put it "polemic" views, figure: (1) the scene of the Jail at Mons; (2) the Cafe in Paris; and (3) the scene on Cyprus. All of these use close-ups of figures who are antagonists to the actor with whom the audience is asked to empathize: the jailer and priest vs. Verlaine, the Parisian crowd vs. Rimbaud, the white guard vs. the slaves and Rimbaud. The caricature is appropriate because it capsules the dramatic conflict embodied in the particular scene. On the whole these uses of caricatured antagonists were felicitous; they certainly pointed the way to the use of caricatured authorities confronting the live actor, Pallenberg, in the role of Schwejk.

The principle of flexibility extended to Piscator's arrangement of the side wings of the triptych screen. During Rimbaud's voyage, only the center screen was used for motion picture projections; two scrims—in front of the set piece and behind it—were also employed to increase the illusion of the movement of the ship. By careful attention to tempo, coordinating acting and the rhythm of the waves, the mood of the scene was underscored; Piscator described the effect: "The fantastic appearance of the ocean and

Rimbaud's hallucinations in his fever aboard the ship are interlocking and become one in tempo, immensity and movement."[11] For the scene of the café in Aden, the stage right wing (representing the sea) was turned back, while the stage left wing was pushed forward: "By his drawing and color, George Grosz puts the near-by environment (cafe, terrace) on the right side and in the center and the more distant environment on the left side in an economical and specific manner."[12] To form Verlaine's cell at Mons the side members were brought forward to shape an enclosure. Bars (not visible in production photos) half-hid the projections. A room was needed once more in the hospital scene at Marseille; again the forward position of the side members of the screen served to surround the hospital bed. The projections were fantastic representations of Africa and Europe, illustrations of Rimbaud's feverish hallucinations as he lay dying. Grosz effectively used a more patterned composition and more childlike line (a return to his own earlier drawing style in the 1915–1918 period) to distinguish the hallucinatory drawings from those indicating a locale.

While the tension between corrupt Europe and primitive Africa was continually exploited in the slides, overt political comment was rare. The most interesting drawing for this aspect is the garret room. The design, in which dark blue-grey walls hold together separate segments, telescopes three events: from right to left, the Commune, explosions above the Paris rooftops, and Verlaine and Rimbaud's sexual relationship. On the right a firing squad shoots three prisoners as a death's head raises his sword. Above is written, "Vive la Kommune." In the center there is the skylight of the garret through which we see explosions in the sky. On the far left a curtain discreetly hides all but two sets of male feet, one within the other. Thus a reference to the homosexual relationship between Verlaine and Rimbaud is incorporated into a representation of revolution. The effect is to be both within and without the room. On the watercolor Grosz scrawled, "feet must be covered." Indeed they were blocked out by a dark shape in the final version as a production photo shows. By eliminating the feet, which were a direct reference to the content of the scene that centered on Mme. Verlaine's realization of the nature of her husband's relationship with Rimbaud, Piscator juxtaposed the psychological action with a seemingly unrelated event, the Commune.

The projections for *Das trunkene Schiff* were experimental undertakings which contributed valuable knowledge of technique to be used in *Schwejk*. When Grosz made drawings for *Schwejk*, he employed fine lines widely separated from one another so that there could be no blurring in the reproduction and projection processes. The *Schwejk* designs are less complex. The earlier drawings were dense in subject matter, perhaps too complicated for an audience to follow. The projections for *Das trunkene Schiff* remained on the screen for periods of minutes, those for *Schwejk* rarely lingered more than a few seconds. Not only the complexity but the poetic function of the majority of the earlier projections differentiates them from the biting editorial gloss of *Schwejk*.

Projections had been used in earlier productions on the German stage, but never before had they been used in such a manner that the artist's hand might directly enter the performance. Using drawings that provided illustrational rather than illusionistic background was an innovation that meant the designer participated more directly in the production than ever before. Piscator's willingness to reshuffle the conventional hierarchy of production elements could not be better demonstrated. He must be credited with a brilliant piece of unconventional "casting": he was perceptive to grasp the analogous relationship between Rimbaud's rejection of a decadent Europe and Grosz's revulsion with German society.

Critical Reaction and Acting

The performance was a triumph for Grosz and for Piscator. The actors received qualified praise, but Paul Zech's play was generally disliked. Hostility to Piscator was channeled into devious routes; Alfred Klaar accused him of deceiving the public about the emptiness of the play by a barrage of technical innovations.[13] Alfred Kerr, who had decided to champion Piscator, interspersed praises for the director among his sharper critical paragraphs; John Heartfield had once caricatured the distinguished critic in a montage which showed Kerr's portrait photograph neatly divided into segments with Roman numerals to their side, a parody of Kerr's own numbered paragraphs in reviews. Kerr had some doubts about the projections, though none about the historical importance of the performance for the integration of actor and projections. He expressed his admiration for the "wonderful" George Grosz, but it annoyed Kerr to think of Grosz's genius in connection with scenes from Rimbaud's life. He apparently felt that he was continually in the artist's studio, being shown Grosz's latest work. For this reason, the most illusionistic scene, that of Rimbaud's voyage on the *Pinguin*, accomplished with actual movie footage and careful play of light on scrim, pleased him far more than the slide projections.[14]

Otto Steinicke, writing for the Communist *Die rote Fahne*,[15] had only praise for Grosz and for Piscator. He took care to point out that the conception of the projections as well as the execution were by Grosz. In connection with the caricature of the jailer at Mons, a design particularly pleasing to Steinicke's Marxist eye, he noted that it resembled a drawing Grosz had contributed to the newspaper earlier that year, and was, as Piscator assured everyone in his article in *Das Kunstblatt*, a symbol of French Imperialism.

Ernst Degner[16] declared that the greatest pleasure of the evening was afforded by Grosz's projections. For once Degner believed Piscator had made a justified use of film! Ernst Heilborn came closest to realizing the implications which the use of projections would have on future performances using "alienation" or distancing effects. He reflectively analyzed the function of the technique: as historical gloss, as polemical visions of participants, as evaluative caricatures of locales. And he thought that through the use of projections, "Zech's play gains . . . something like a perspective, something like a commentary."[17]

So accurate was this analysis that Heilborn realized the consequences of these functions: to undercut or at least diminish the importance of the words. This deviated from his idea of verbal theatre, and he was not prepared to accept so radical a departure.

Whatever one's opinion of the technical innovations and their suitability, there remained the play. It was not the sort of piece in which an actor could achieve an independently brilliant performance; the cast struggled with the inherent faults of the text as well as the particular problems raised by the incorporation of projected scenery and live actors.[18] Ernst Degner made, perhaps, the most bitter indictment of the play's psychological bent: "Paul Zech was not capable of developing this fate towards its great tragedy. The whining during the scenes between Rimbaud and Verlaine seemed to be more of an outbreak of female hysterics."[19] Ernst Heilborn was equally contemptuous of the "tragic" relationship which occupied more than half the play, "Here we do not see soulful torture and ecstasy, it is all plain fuss."[20]

There were only two roles of real importance, and both Carl Achaz as Rimbaud and Leonard Steckel as Verlaine had to sustain long passages of intense, poetic language. Critics were divided as to their success. Afred Kerr pointed out Achaz's resemblance to the Fantin-Latour portrait of Rimbaud. He thought Rimbaud should be "cooler" than the continually raving Achaz. Klaar, on the other hand, liked Achaz's ability to maintain intensity: "Carl Ludwig Achaz played Rimbaud with temperamental youthfulness and showed an ongoing vocal strength that did justice to all audacious paradoxes and all the tortures during his fever hallucinations."[21] Klaar's animosity was reserved for Piscator, the confused action and stilted language of the play. Steinicke was enthusiastic about the young cast: he singled out Rimbaud's death for its majesty: "How he lunges again at the little priest's throat before he collapses is grand."[22] Leonard Steckel, who had played the pawnbroker in the Grosz-designed production of *Nebeneinander* and who was to be among the first of Piscator's actors to return to perform with Brecht's Berliner Ensemble after the war, labored against overwhelming odds in his portrayal of the older and more sentimental poet. To his credit he drew praise from all the critics. Wolfgang Zeller's music was helpful in sustaining the rapidly changing moods. The period costumes were neglected by the critics.

Only a few months before the May production of *Das trunkene Schiff*,

Brecht had directed his own *Baal* for the Deutsches Theater. The similarities with the Zech play are superficial: they both deal with bisexual poets who reject European civilization for a wild, even absurd, nature. But *Baal* has none of the linguistic liabilities of *Das trunkene Schiff*. Fortunately the technical innovations used in staging the latter were about to be applied to the production of a script constructed in large part by Brecht.

The Adventures of the Good Soldier Schwejk

The third and most successful production which Grosz designed for Piscator was a synthesis of techniques which had been only partially effective in earlier productions, plus a few new devices and several strong talents new to the Piscator stage. Critics praised *The Adventures of the Good Soldier Schwejk*, even while censuring its profanation of army, state, and church. The public enthusiastically endorsed the production with laughter and applause. *Schwejk* ranks among the 10 or so most important productions during the Weimar Republic, not solely for its technical innovations or fine acting, but also for the change in comic sensibility which the play embodied. It was new, not the face-lifting à la Jessner of a classic nor a conventional play onto which Piscator grafted a social message and historical context. As the director observed, the popular novel from which the dramatization was constructed presented the fate of a simple man caught in the events of his time rather than the plight of a genius, like Zech's life of Rimbaud.[23] The adaptation of Jaroslav Hasek's satire took more than a year and brought together four of the Republic's major talents—Brecht, Pallenberg, Piscator, and Grosz—in their most successful collaboration.

Beginning on the day of the assassination of Archduke Ferdinand, the picaresque adventures of the dog merchant, Schwejk, continue through the early years of the war. The focus moves with the hapless Schwejk from the red tape of the bureaucratic officialdom of Prague under the Austrian hegemony to the everyday life of the soldier and on to the hardships of the front lines. Guileless or possessed by a strange cunning, Schwejk, certified feeble-minded in his previous military service, enthusiastically accepts the tenets of the Austrian State and in doing so undermines army, monarchy, and church. Piscator interpreted Schwejk's character as such an asocial force that even in a Communist society he would dissolve institutions. The passive Schwejk, like Lazarillo de Tormes, changes masters several times, but remains true to his own personal code of survival. He is the modern antiheroic protagonist, whose heroism consists of circumventing the system, whose solution to almost any scrape is an anecdote.

Hasek died before completing his novel, and the task of finishing the work was left to a gentleman named Vanck. Max Brod and Hans Reimann received the rights to threatrical adaptation. Rather than follow the episodic nature of the picaresque account, Brod and Reimann attempted to construct a conventionally well-made play about the central figure of Schwejk. This comedy, which Piscator called a "pseudo-comic farce," marred by a conventional ending, was offered to Piscator and rejected by him. In the same month and year that Piscator presented his *Schwejk*, January, 1928, the Stadttheater of Düsseldorf presented a version more faithful to the Brod-Reimann adaptation.

With Leo Lania, Gasbarra, and Brecht, and with frequent advice from Grosz, Piscator set out to work on his own adaptation which he hoped to present as a *fait accompli* to the owners of the adaptation patent. Several problems were manifest: there were far too many episodes, anecdotes, and characters for a three-hour, theatrical presentation; parts of the translation by Grete Reiner used Prague-dialect German and Hungarian; the free-flowing nature of the text had somehow to be preserved on stage; the narrative comments of the author, frequently tacit comparisons to the heroic stance of earlier warriors, had to be assimilated into a theatrical form of story telling. Piscator jokingly suggested that the adaptation be presented on five successive nights. He later planned to continue the adventures in a second production, but Brod and Reimann, getting wind of his plans, squelched them. Although concerning events then ten or more years old, the novel surged with modernity which Piscator was fearful of losing in the transfer to the stage; as the Weimar Republic accelerated its military and paramilitary rearmament, the antimilitaristic thesis of *Schwejk* maintained relevancy. Examining Brecht's typescript and comments, Pavel Petr has speculated that the bulk of the "Piscator" adaptation was actually written by Brecht.[24] Piscator, on the other hand, cites instances of specific suggestions and modifications which point to a collaboration in the most complete sense. Readers familiar with the novel would have no difficulty in recognizing Schwejk and his adventures, although characters were at times combined and there were, infrequently, modifications in the psychology of the protagonist, usually making him more active and more consciously a comedian. Brecht called the adaptation a "pure montage of the novel."[25]

Piscator conceived of the movement of the play as representing Schwejk's passivity before a flood of events. To implement this interpretation he thought of conveyor belts which permitted rapid changes of properties, as well as comic movements by actors. The mechanical movement of the conveyor belts was intrinsically comic; their passengers could only prove Bergson's thesis that man forced to move as a machine was funny. The treadmills, along with the use of projections, permitted Piscator and his collaborators to render the adaptation in episodic form, though the number of episodes in the novel still had to be drastically curtailed. The film, which will be discussed further in examining Grosz's designs, served a variety of purposes and included both specially photographed shots of Prague streets and other landscapes made by Hübler-Kahla and animated sequences by Grosz.

Still another innovation was employed: cutout figures, larger than life size, much like Grosz's shields for *Methusalem*. Piscator had originally entertained the idea of reducing the cast to a single "live" actor as Schwejk. Projections and the two-dimensional figures would then have acted the roles of Schwejk's antagonists. Another idea, considered and rejected, was a schematic use of cutouts and film to represent the ideological divisions within the play. These notions were modified, so that roles which might have been considered supernumeraries in conventional productions were filled by the cutouts, while many of the authoritarian figures whom Schwejk encountered were represented on the screen, tremendously enlarged, in close-up drawings by Grosz. The furnishings of the stage were stripped to a bare minimum: two parallel conveyor belts capable of moving at will in both directions were placed parallel to the footlights. To either side a single flat served as masking, and across the back of the stage a drop for projections completed the basic setting. On this basically architectural stage a seemingly endless succession of different "stage pictures" passed. The adaptation was divided into two parts by a single intermission. The first half contained 14 scenes which necessitated about 11 locales. The second act was divided into four major scenes, and each of these was subdivided into as many as three locations. Set pieces or large properties, accompanied by "editorial" comment in the projections were used to suggest the locations.

Synopsis of the Adaptation

Schwejk and his charlady, Frau Müller, discuss the assassination of Archduke Ferdinand (I, i) and once he understands which Ferdinand has been killed and under what circumstances, Schwejk leaves the flats which represent his room and hurries off to the tavern (or rather, in the Piscator production, the tavern trundles toward Schwejk on the conveyor) where he may ruminate on the events of the day.

At the Flagon (I, ii) he encounters a new customer, the police spy, Brettschneider, who craftily attempts to trap Schwejk and the proprietor, Palivec, into self-incriminatory statements. The best he gets from Schwejk is, "You can't replace Ferdinand with just any damned fool." The intrepid Brettschneider manages to invent charges against both the consciously tight-lipped Palivec, who has nevertheless removed a fly-specked portrait of the emperor, and the guilelessly innocent but talkative Schwejk.

Schwejk and his captor move off toward the police headquarters. Several episodes concerning his first imprisonment are now deleted which appear in the action of the novel; Schwejk recounts them instead when he returns home to converse with Frau Müller and discover his mobilization papers (I, iii). As a result, the old lady must push the rheumatic volunteer to induction headquarters in a wheel chair (I, iv); along the way they meet a parade of the cutout figures (Plates 27–29). The 16 cutout figures of newspaper readers that Grosz designed form an impressive human comedy of Berlin (more than Prague) types. Schwejk's heroism, as he screams, "on to Belgrade," will lead to the admiration of a Baroness who visits Schwejk in the hospital.

Meanwhile at the induction headquarters (I, v), Dr. Bautze, chairman of the board of medical examiners, a man possessed with a pathological hatred of malingerers, orders an already dead recruit to be on his way, thus duplicating the gag in one of Grosz's most famous prints, "Fit for Active Service" (1922). Nor does Schwejk escape the doctor's perpetually optimistic diagnosis; he is ordered off to the infirmary for a quick cure.

The method in this establishment is to make the cure more unendurable than the disease. Scenes within the hospital (I, vi) closely follow the dialogue of the novel (Plate 31). Dr. Bautze, the sadistic chief of the medical staff, interrogates Schwejk, promising him instant cure with clyster, quinine, stomach pump, and starvation diet, the methods universally successful with his unfortunate patients. Next the Baroness von Botzenheim comes to reward the gallantry of the rheumatic cripple who has so bravely volunteered, a story widely publicized in the pro-Austrian press. When she remarks that he will soon be at the front, Piscator's Schwejk, unlike Hasek's, chokes on the delicacies she has brought him. The terrible doctor (Plate 30) catches his patients eating the tidbits the Baroness has bestowed on them, and sentences them to have their stomachs pumped (Plate 32). Producing too much tongue, Schwejk is accused of intentional mockery by the inspecting doctors. His excuses that he is only following orders are met with fury, and fury, and Schwejk is sent off to the detention barracks (Plate 33). He sings as he walks on the treadmill (I, vii):

> Tho't, serving nothing but a rush
> Thought it would last
> A week or a fortnight-
> And be over with.[26]

At the detention barracks (I, viii) Schwejk joins a group of idealists and nonidealists who have stolen or committed other offenses in order to avoid active duty. The guards, headed by Captain Slawik, treat their unwilling guests brutishly. In this bleak atmosphere, one of the prisoners' few diversions is the weekly sermon of the convert priest and sometime *bon vivant*, Otto Katz. He is attracted to Schwejk, the only prisoner who cries during his preaching. The others, attired in long underwear, scratch lice and play cards, while the chaplain spews forth militaristic propaganda; in the production the listeners, except Schwejk, were represented by large cutouts (Plate 34).

Later (I, viii) Schwejk endears himself further to the priest by confessing that his tears are sham. Otto Katz becomes Schwejk's master, but the hilarious adventures of the priest who tipples and his orderly are largely omitted from the theatrical production. Instead, the chaplain almost immediately loses Schwejk in a card game to the ladies-man Lt. Lukasch (I, ix).

In another scene at the lieutenant's (I, x) his new master learns of Schwejk's experience in animal dealing when the cat eats the lieutenant's canary. He decides that Schwejk shall find a new pet, a dog. Schwejk also becomes involved in one of Lukasch's frequent amorous intrigues. A married lady, Kati, in flight from her husband, drops in unexpectedly on the lieutenant. Schwejk, instructed to carry out her every wish while his master remains on duty, complies with one not strictly anticipated by Lukasch.

In the next four scenes (I, xi–xiv) several incidents which are more or less distinct in the novel are brought into a closer relationship. Lukasch, as a jealous Kati lies in bed, sends Schwejk off with a mysterious letter and in search of the dog (xi). With his pal Woditschka, Schwejk opens Lukasch's letter to Frau Etelka Baranyi (Kakonyi, in Hasek's version). In this way, the lieutenant's amorous feelings for the lady he has seen at the theatre are explained to the audience. As Petr remarks, the opening of the letter is a remarkable departure from the character of Hasek's Schwejk, who does not intentionally meddle in his master's life.[27] The pals steal a dog from the officer's maid, as Blahnik does alone in the novel. Blahnik and Woditschka, distinct characters in Hasek's novel, are compressed in the character of Woditschka, just as the incidents of Kati's visit, the theft of the dog, and the attempted rendezvous with Etelka, are compressed in the following scenes. Woditschka and Schwejk then go to the Baranyi house with the dog (sc. xiii). As in the novel, the irate Hungarian husband objects to his wife's receiving notes from amorous swains and a brawl ensues. Schwejk and Woditschka bid each other farewell to meet "at six o'clock after the war" and go off to either side. Back at the barracks yard (I, xiv) the officer, talking with Lukasch as Schwejk comes up with the dog, recognizes his pet. The furious captain berates Lukasch for his amorous adventures and for the theft of the dog; as a result Lukasch and Schwejk are sent to the front.

The second half of the evening moves closer to the frontlines as Lukasch and Schwejk travel to Budweis (II, i). Several of the adventures in traveling are incorporated from the novel, such as the incident of the lost luggage, General von Schwarzburg's tongue lashing, and Schwejk's unfortunate experimentation with the emergency brake. Lukasch allows his subordinate to be removed from the train at Tabor, after he has halted the train unexpectedly, to be sent on to Budweis by foot.

The "Budweiser Anabasis," in which Schwejk attempts to catch up with his regiment on foot, was divided into two scenes. In the first (II, ii, a) Schwejk meets an old woman who takes him for a fugitive from the police and gives directions accordingly. Schwejk, of course, falls into hands of the paranoid sheriff (II, ii, b). After interrogation and various confusions, Schwejk is eventually sent on to his regiment by train.

Piscator's stage directions give the best idea of how the complicated wanderings were made clear:

> Scenery from the right. A town appears. Policemen are seen through the map on the screen. Scenery from the left. A town. The map shows Schwejk making a wide detour around the town. Film: railroad tracks, signal lamps, a watchman's shanty, gates at a crossing, and then the highway. On the left the lights of Tabor can be seen. The lights travel along for a stretch, keeping pace and shifting toward the middle, slip back into the distance, then disappear entirely as if behind a hill. In the background the night sky, against which a hilly, wooded landscape is silhouetted dimly. Fade into a map showing Budweis. The titles point out Schwejk's direction. The following caption appears on the map (white print): Xenophon, a general of ancient times, hastened across all of Asia Minor, without maps and ended up God knows where. A continuous march in a straight line is called an anabasis ... Far away, somewhere north on the Gallic Sea, Caesar's legions, which had gotten there also without the aid of maps, decided to return to Rome by a route different from the one by which they came. Since then it has been said that all roads lead to Budweis—something which Schwejk fully believed. And the devil only knows how it happened that instead of going south to Budweis, Schwejk marched in a straight line west. . . .[28]

In custody in a military transport with other hungry soldiers, Schwejk sleeps in the straw (III, iii, a). On his return to the regiment (III, iii, b) Lt. Biegler (whose character is a fusion of Biegler and Dub in the novel) greets Schwejk as a deserter from the regiment. Lukasch reproaches him with the separation from his beloved Etelka (in the novel Lukasch is merely attracted to Etelka in an extremely brief episode; Brod and Reimann built the love intrigue into a major theme). Marek, a déclassé intellectual in Piscator's dramatization, and Baloun, the glutton who cannot find enough to eat, were introduced in these sequences. Baloun's pilfering and punishment provided the humor of these scenes within the car, behind it on the tracks, and behind the departing wagon.

How could the finale of these humorous adventures be found? Hasek had died without terminating the novel. Brod and Reimann had halted the play with the engagement of Lt. Lukasch and his beloved Etelka. It was a conventional ending that did not deviate from the expectations of centuries of comedy-goers. The various alternatives for an ending are important for they demonstrate a change in comic sensibility.

Throughout the collaboration George Grosz had trumpeted a more ferocious note than most of his colleagues. It was he who wished the performance to be, not simply a social satire, but a biting indictment of war.

His drawings and two-dimensional cutouts portrayed the lunatic authorities of the Austrian state, and their tone was far from the understated attack by Hasek. For the denouement, Grosz proposed a scene of total destruction. The surroundings are in ruins; there is a comic "knock about" or the *dramatis personae*, costumed as skeletons and wearing death's heads, drink to their own health.[29]

Leo Lania had still another suggestion, less macabre and more ironic than Grosz's.[30] At the end of the war, waiting at the tavern for Sapper Woditschka, Schwejk meets police detective Brettschneider in place of his old friend. Schwejk is arrested again; the old Austria continues.

For a time, Lania's ending seemed the most appropriate. Piscator, however, discovered another passage which seemed to reiterate the unending conflict with authority, as Lania's did, but that would also extend the satire to still other areas. In an extremely brief passage of the novel, Lt. Biegler, the officious and extremely green officer, dreams that he has reached heaven:

> Then he was in a motor car which, as the result of an explosion, reached the gates of heaven, for which the password was "God and Kaiser." He was admitted to the presence of God who turned out to be none other than Captain Sagner, who was accusing him of masquerading as a major general. Then he foundered into a new dream.[31]

Out of this slender description grew Schwejk's theatrical apotheosis. In heaven Schwejk would continue to prove authority as pompous and inhuman as in its terrestrial manifestations. Piscator proposed the finale; Brod enthusiastically accepted it, and Gasbarra wrote the scene. George Grosz caricatured God as a gouty old general; senility was evident in every crease of the feeble officer seated on his cloud.

Before this god paraded the invalids and the maimed of the war: 20 of the cutout marionette invalids drawn by Grosz, some real invalids—one who trails his intestines, another who carries his leg under his arm, a third who wears his head on his arm. Others carried human parts in knapsacks; everything was covered with blood and mud. Finally two little girls with bloodied faces, hand in hand, filed by. The procession moved to the blare of the Radetsky March.

The effect, which outdid the macabre humor of Grosz's proposals, was simply too strong for the public. As Piscator says, the march of the maimed was "unbearable." Only at the rehearsal reserved for the Special Section of the Volksbühne did the cripples and mutilated march.

In the ensuing pinch, the scene proposed by Brod was reconsidered and discarded because it had not been properly rehearsed. The proposal of Schwejk's farewell to Woditschka and the agreement to meet "at six after the world war" was substituted.

Another ending was discarded apparently without ever being performed. The novel closes as Schwejk is taken prisoner by the Hungarians who, naturally enough, are suspicious of the Russian uniform he has purloined from a soldier taking a dip. The ending of the Brecht typescript and several Grosz drawings for animated film merged this sequence with the explosion of a grenade that kills the protagonist.

Separated from the regiment, Marek and Schwejk look about for the battlefield; as Schwejk continues to chatter, justifying the war, Marek decamps, leaving Schwejk to his own patriotic slogans. On the screen a Grosz drawing showing the Russian soldier in the midst of a pond is projected. By conveyor belt, a bush arrives with the clothing of the Russian neatly laid out. Delighted, Schwejk tries it on for size, but at that moment a Hungarian patrol pounces upon him. As Schwejk protests that he is on their side, a shell explodes and the good soldier falls.

Mordecai Gorelik describes the final effects achieved with Grosz's projections

> From the upper corner of the screen a procession of crosses starts toward the audience. As the crosses growing nearer in perspective reach the lower edge of the screen, a muslin drop, lowered downstage catches them once more, bringing them still closer to the spectators. A rain of crosses falls upon this wry comedy as the lights begin to go up. . . .[32]

The ending finally adopted does seem more in keeping with Hasek's satire than the grotesque horror show originally used. So excited and confused was the projectionist by the various modifications in the space of a few days that he forgot to open the lens for the first performance that was supposed to have ended with the crosses. The rain of crosses, the reassertion of man's mortality, commanded the audience to go beyond laughter to reflection.

Siegfried Kracauer has taken up the theme of rebellion as it was treated by film artists in the Weimar Republic. Plays such as *Methusalem*, *Nebeneinander*, and *Kanzlist Krehler* support his thesis. *Wandlung* deals with a more successful rebellion because the solution can be stated in the vaguest humanistic terms; authority is simply replaced with a higher authority called humanity. The character of Schwejk, a direct opposite to the conscious rebel, Friedrich in *Wandlung*, takes this futility of rebellion one step further; for Schwejk, it is impossible either to rebel or to comply with corrupt authority. No better proof can be given of the change in comic sensibility than an account of the successive versions in the adaptation of the novel *Schwejk*. Brod and Reimann offered an ending which would have been acceptable to the sensibility of the Old Regime. All of the proposals, except Lania's, included reference to death. Piscator's collaborative adaptation heightened Hasek's theme: the mocking of corrupt authority by Schwejk's ready compliance.

Grosz's Designs

On the whole, Grosz was the spokesman for ferocity in the collaboration, as Brod and Reimann were advocates of insipidity. The primary function of the projections for *Das trunkene Schiff* had been to provide indications of locale; the principal function of the *Schwejk* projections and cutouts was to provide caricatured views of Schwejk's antagonists. Grosz was given, in effect, free rein to make editorial comment. Animated film replaced live actors frequently. A tertiary role for the projections was in providing scenery; for the most part set pieces moving across the stage on the conveyors were signposts to locale. In certain sequences where Piscator wished to use photographs of landscapes, Grosz drawings were interpolated in editing the movie footage, so that there was an alternation of real trees, for instance, and those drawn by Grosz.

Piscator has described the manner in which Hübler-Kahla's naturalistic film (he also went to Prague for location shots of the streets) was edited and incorporated with animated sequences in the Budweis Anabasis:

> And finally I tried to combine naturalistic film with cartoon for the march to Budéjovice and for the final battle scenes. In the "Anabasis" scene I had clumps of trees drawn on the pictures which flowed past; this brought out very strongly the notion of continuity and the hopelessness of the march. In the intervals between scenes this film led quite naturally into the drawn projections.[33]

Grosz's drawings were a substitute for the narrator's voice in the novel. Gasbarra has pointed out this function of Grosz's graphic editorials:

> At the beginning of each chapter where Hasek made direct general comments on his theme, Piscator projected cartoons, drawn by George Grosz. In this way he could effectively condense the forces which were opposed to Schwejk.[34]

In order to portray the verbal rationalization of the evils of the establishment, Grosz developed an animated symbol. The paragraph sign first appears in Grosz's stage designs in the setting of the police station in *Nebeneinander*, where it is co-equal with the eagle and the gibbet in symbolizing the forces of the state. Again, in *Das trunkene Schiff*, the sign appeared next to the raving priest in the projection for Verlaine's cell at Mons. It is doubtful that the symbol was much noticed in these early instances, as it was not activated until *Schwejk*. In *Schwejk* the paragraph symbol was placed in contexts which made its meaning unmistakable. At the beginning of the evening, for instance, a drawing was projected in which two figures, with gramophone horns for heads and waving flags, shout jingoistic slogans at each other as they scurry over a cloud of paragraph signs. In an animated sequence a simple and ornamental tree changes its branches and trunk into paragraph signs from which hang numerous bodies (Plate 35). Or the dome of a simpleton's head is flung open and out fly the paragraphs. A projection which was apparently intended for the final sequences shows a prostrate skeleton in boots. Above the supine form is an enormous paragraph sign which supports a radiant monarchical crown.

The scenes of the detention barracks (I, viii) illustrate well the function of Grosz's drawings as surrogates for Hasek's narrative descriptions. Hasek's narrative tacitly compares the guards to brutes, and this was illustrated with a series of drawings in which the jailers are actually transformed into bloodthirsty dogs (Plate 36). Costuming was also exaggerated to reinforce the point: the chief jailer, Slawik, wore an enormous fist.

The horrors of Dr. Bautze's infirmary were matters which Grosz, having lived through similar experiences, felt most vividly. In this sequence the torturing of prisoners under the guise of medical treatment, would have been a difficult, and perhaps repulsive, bit of stage action. The terrified expression of the victim (Plate 32), the preparation of the clyster and the use of the stomach pump were outrages which could be shown in close-up range through Grosz's drawings, and, in this case, the drawings provided a necessary distance and made credible that which would have been incredible or revolting on stage.

The series of drawings in which Grosz analyzed the facial transitions of the rage of Dr. Bautze (Plate 30) mark a new function for projections, as the antagonist to the live actor. Acting must respond in a style partially determined by the variation in size of the auditorium and particularly the distance separating audience and stage. In the Bautze sequence, the doctor's apoplectic face was projected onto the back screen; the solitary figure of Schwejk faced this formidable set of spare lines mobilely shaping themselves into the grimaces and contortions of anger. In a medium-sized theatre, such as the Nollendorfplatz (capacity 1,106) an actor could not rely on his facial expression carrying. Grosz's drawing subsumed all but the voice of the actor. It was a distillation and analysis of the actor's art that provided the perfect example of Brecht's notion that the actor should report an emotion rather than giving the illusion of experiencing the emotion on stage. The artificial reconstruction of the exterior manifestations of anger drove home the distinction between the flesh and blood Schwejk, played by Pallenberg, and his inhuman antagonists. Like the conveyor belts, and virtually every other bit of scenery in the presentation, Grosz's drawings are liberated from the conventional role of background material to the performers and raised to the level of active participants in the drama. Within this antiillusionistic context, Grosz could give free rein to his penchant for caricature; it became a virtue rather than a liability.

Besides this gift for capturing types, Grosz brought a sense of contemporaneity to the performance; his drawings, like all art, had an existence outside of conventional time; by their vivacity, a quality separate from the mortal, time-bound energies of the performers and from the historical context of the First World War, these drawings aided in freeing the performance from contingencies of history, or so Piscator thought when he wrote:

> Grosz' main achievement in this film was not simply his inspired delineation of the types. He managed in this film to extract Schwejk or rather Schwejk's world from its historical period and establish a link with the present. The medical officers, officers, public prosecutors were figures that are still alive today in Prussia/Germany. And so the play carried on the struggle on the political level of the day.[35]

If Piscator felt that Grosz had provided a vital link with contemporary art, and hence contemporary politics, Grosz thought Piscator had provided a drawing board which could be used by all young artists:

> So for the graphic artist Erwin simply erected a huge drawing board covered with white paper at the back of the stage, and on this I accompany the action and underline malicious comments and asides. Erwin has in fact opened up a vast new field for graphic art, a sort of draftsman's circus . . . Here the Daumiers of today can issue their warning and paint terror on the walls. What a medium for any artist who wants to speak directly to the masses. Of course a new drawing surface requires new methods, a new economical language of line—a real chance to educate woolly minds and chaotic hands! The line has to be photogenic-clear simple, not too thin (in case of over-exposure) and hard, like the drawings and wood cuts in Gothic block books and the lapidary engravings on the Pyramids.[36]

Like all good satirists Grosz hoped to offend and welcomed furor as proof of efficacy. It is curious, however, that he was indicted not for his projections for *Schwejk*, rather for the inexpensive, and therefore widely distributed portfolio, *Hintergrund* published by Herzfelde. These small lithographs were taken from Grosz's drawings for the *Schwejk* projections. One of these caused particular outrage: Christ in a gas mask with the provocative caption, "SHUT UP AND SOLDIER ON." There can be little doubt that Grosz wished to indict the Church for its tacit advocacy of World War I. In other of the *Schwejk* drawings the Church was compared with other authorities, the monarchy and the military, as advocates of war. Considering the Katz episodes in Hasek's novel, Grosz can scarcely be accused of introducing the theme gratuitously. He was tried and fined for blasphemy; the ruling was reversed by a higher court the following year. It seemed to matter little that Hasek had been just as blasphemous and anticlerical in his novel, which was indeed prohibited by certain groups, such as the army, but which was not banned. The prosecution of Grosz by the Weimar Republic for blasphemy was a fairly obvious case of displacement: he was prosecuted for blasphemy but this was not really his offense; rather he had erred in ridiculing values and a political regime which many citizens of the Weimar Republic continued to believe represented the "true" Germany.

In all Grosz made some 300 drawings for *Schwejk*; of these about 30 may have been for the cutout figures. These two-dimensional, painted representations were most frequently used in place of the distracting supernumeraries who would have crowded the stage. The impressive massing of supernumeraries had grown with the rise of naturalism in the theatre. Before that in eighteenth- and nineteenth-century scenography, the "extra" had frequently been a painted figure on a backdrop. In both cases, the painted or real extras had been used to extend the illusion; in the case of Grosz's cutouts the purpose was quite the opposite: anti-illusionism. In the jargon which has grown up to explain Brecht's distinctive stagings, this would be called a *Verfremdungseffekt*. The cutout idea grew very naturally out of Grosz's constructivist designs for *Methusalem*. Its use has since been duplicated on the German and American stages. While acknowledging their anti-illusionistic function, it is well to remember that they served a practical purpose. Grosz carefully accentuated the grotesquerie of the listeners to Katz's sermon (Plate 34). A group of actors assembled before the Chaplain, writhing and scratching lice and playing cards behind their backs, would have distracted attention from the principals, Katz and Schwejk. The cutouts permitted the Nollendorfplatz audience to focus upon the content of Katz's jingoistic sermon, and Schwejk's tearful reaction. Similarly, at other points in the action where the cutouts were employed, they set off the live actors in an unnatural scale. It would be ridiculous to accuse Brecht of stealing ideas from a production on which he was an intimate collaborator. On the other hand, the theory of *Verfremdungseffekt* has become so overly intellectualized that it would be good to remember that the effects themselves were often not invented by Brecht, but grew quite naturally out of earlier productions, such as the projections for *Das trunkene Schiff* and the cutouts planned for *Methusalem* in 1922, and that these devices reached fruition, and hence coherent use, in *Schwejk* several years before Brecht began to use them systematically as principles of dramaturgy. Even such standard devices as the projected signboard (see Plate 33, the "title" for the detention barracks scene) were employed, as Brecht had already done in several plays.

Another important element in the production, which would be used for later "epic" stagings, was the pair of moving sidewalks. The conveyor belts were large: 2.7 m. wide, 17 m. long and about 40 cm. high. Even more staggering was the weight: about 5,000 kilos. In order to install the belts for rehearsals, the heavy hemisphere employed for *Rasputin* had to be removed, the bands brought in. The revolving stage was useful in transporting these heavy scenic elements; nevertheless, the installation of the conveyor belts took 16 men two hours; later, with practice, this was reduced to 45 minutes.

It was largely because of such costly and complicated scene shifts that Piscator had less than two weeks' rehearsal with the belts: they were first installed January 8; the production opened January 23. The elaborate machinery was related both to theatre economy and acting style, which will be discussed in a moment. An average house at the Nollendorfplatz theatre (a smaller theatre constructed in the architectural style of a court theatre, and therefore more difficult to work with, despite its acoustics, which were better than the Bülowplatz) would yield 3,000–3,500 marks;[37] so great a success was the *Schwejk* production that the yield was between 7–9,000 marks per evening.[38] It was the desire to exploit this success which led Piscator, who no longer had the valuable support of the Volksbühne subscribers although the theatre had its own subscription system, to overextend himself by acquiring another theatre, the Lessing. When Pallenberg decided to leave *Schwejk* in April, several months before Piscator had thought that he would, for a South American tour, the doom of the Piscator stages in Berlin was sealed.

Max Pallenberg and Acting Style

There is a logic in the development of and interaction between production elements of this presentation which might escape the casual spectator. The preservation of the "epic" form of the novel, and of Schwejk's passive nature, led Piscator to the solution of treadmills and film; the scenic means engendered, intentionally and accidentally, a distinctive playing style. The disparity between what Max Pallenberg, a star who commanded a top salary at the time of Schwejk, an actor schooled by Reinhardt, might have been expected to do and what he actually did was largely determined by the scenic format. Under these scenic conditions Reinhardt's technique of acting was not only impossible but also undesirable. The model for much of the performance was the early Charlie Chaplin. Chaplin had been at the back of Piscator's mind from the first: "And for the whole thing I had in mind a sort of knockabout style, reminiscent of Chaplin or Vaudeville."[39]

On the disastrously unintentional side were the treadmills which at first threatened to annul the performance. So noisy were they at the first rehearsal that actors could not be heard. Piscator collapsed in helpless laughter. With the aid of Richter's ingenuity felt, soap, and graphite and some heavy reinforcement of the floorboards, the noise of the machinery was diminished. Actors still had to speak in a half-shout, and such a register could only have eliminated many subtleties of inflection normally connected with illusionistic psychological portrayal. The style was, perforce, presentational. To Pallenberg's credit he was able to overcome his anxieties, fears that were rather well justified considering the roar of the machinery and the tendency for properties to fall down on the belts, without the illusionistic properties and background to which he had been accustomed.

Reinhardt was of course too varied and too great to be classified under one rubric; his prompt books, however, show careful attention to facial expression and gesture. In the Kammerspiele every nuance of psychological portraiture could be felt by the audience. Stress was laid on ensemble playing in which the actor must relate, not to his audience, but to his counterparts in their fictitious identities and in a manner consistent with the character the actor is playing. In such essentially realistic acting, eyes could not stray nor could an actor preempt his comrades. In *Schwejk* this unity of tone was purposefully discarded. Frequently Pallenberg was the only "live" actor on stage. His antagonists were actual voices accompanying projected images. Schwejk had to react to these images as if they were real people. The audience was asked to accept the convention of the caricatured image as human, but always to keep in mind the principle of the artifice. Schwejk undermines these images of authority by compliance, not by making the authorities incredible or denying their reality. Hence Pallenberg continued to play an illusionistic role, but under conditions in which all of the properties and most of the human relationships used normally to support the actor's art of illusion were discarded.

Physically Pallenberg was well endowed to play the role of Schwejk. Fascinated with the actor's broad grin, George Grosz made several drawings of the actor; one of these was included in *Hintergrund* and also used for the poster (Plate 37). Pallenberg had a fleshy, mobile face; the bulb of his squarish nose and his long upper lip seemed parts of a comic mask. Most importantly, he could grin in a way which was at once benign and slightly idiotic and also consciously mocking; cover his eyes in a photograph and the visage is harmless; cover the mouth and Pallenberg's eyes mock you. He was short and bulky; his loose fitting uniform, with its too large hat and protruding visor, accentuated his identity as tramp-clown.

The principal modification in the adaptation of novel to stage had been the stress upon Schwejk's involvement in the affairs of Lt. Lukasch, a role as conventional and time-honored as the clever Plautine slave's endeavors in behalf of his amorous master. The question was "Is Schwejk conscious or a complete idiot?" In the novel the question could remain unanswered more easily. On stage it was more difficult to maintain the ambivalence and on the whole Pallenberg had to play the role with greater slyness, to exaggerate ironies. Piscator captured the need to embody a paradox in the role: "This was Schwejk's significance: he was not just a clown whose antics ultimately affirm the state of things, but a grand skeptic whose rigid, untiring affirmation of reality reduces reality to nullity."[40]

Pallenberg instrumented his interpretation of Schwejk as a more conscious clown with gestures, not unlike Chaplin's, which were too refined for the character of the peasant Schwejk in the novel. As Petr points out, such graceful movement was essentially a contradiction to the nature of Hasek's protagonist, but many minor alterations in the character of Schwejk justified the greater elegance and consciousness Pallenberg brought to the role.[41]

Piscator thought Pallenberg's creation would be recorded as one of the immortal ones in the history of the theatre. Quite a few critics stated tacitly what Franz Servaes said explicitly; the best reason for the adaptation was the role it afforded Pallenberg.[42] To Kurt Kersten, Pallenberg's Schwejk could only be compared to such universal characters, suffering and genuinely naive, as Candide and Eulenspiegel.[43]

"In the evening Piscator's *Schwejk*. Pallenberg is in charge of the whole thing, genre comedy, very effective. But the best part of the book does not come across—the things one reads between the lines, the intimate details. In the play one finds clever snatches of barracks style; some of the scenic effects are simply bad, actually a comedown from the first play (the Toller),[44] Schlemmer wrote to his wife. It would be difficult to think of a more devoted formalist than Schlemmer, and there is little wonder that he disliked the presentation. He also wasn't fond of Grosz. In addition he was angling through his connection with Walter Gropius for the job of Traugott Müller, Piscator's staff designer. Other members of the audience were more likely to be influenced by critics.

Critical Reaction

What would a reader of 10 or so of the more important Berlin dailies have been advised about the quality of the *Schwejk* presentation? The hypothetical reader would have had to be as passive as the feebleminded Schwejk to accept the reviews at face value. It is not surprising that in a partial survey the polarities of opinion are represented by Otto Steinicke, who wrote for the Communist *Die rote Fahne*, and Franz Servaes, who wrote for Hugenberg's Nationalist *Lokalanzeiger*. The hypothetical reader would have been assured that he must see *Schwejk* for Pallenberg's performance; on this point there was general agreement. All of the reviewers realized that something new had been brought into the theatre. The significance of the "epic" staging of satire eluded most. The question was rather whether conveyor belts and film were more effective devices than those in other Piscator productions. The issue of art vs. propaganda lurked behind every phrase: could one really enjoy *Schwejk* for Pallenberg's performance while ignoring the antimilitaristic thesis? The easiest method of rationalization was to split the production into halves. Using this gambit, Monty Jacobs traced the division in "humor" and "hate" from Hasek's novel to the theatrical presentation: Pallenberg represented the humorous; Grosz and Piscator the hate. Further obfuscation could be achieved by prolonged discussion of the changes in Hasek's *Schwejk*. Everyone realized the character was different on stage, but no one admitted the role his own imagination as a reader of the novel had played in creating the "Hasek" Schwejk. The matter of the rival adaptations could also be enlarged upon, and since every issue was sensitized politically, there were moral censures to be made depending on which side of the political spectrum the writer stood.

Was the theatre enriched by the new techniques? It was necessary, of course, to define theatre and to decide if the techniques were genuinely new. Monty Jacobs thought so:

> An experiment, not quite fully developed, but a promising one, courageous breaking of new ground. Theatre like this makes man the master and not the slave of machinery. . . . Those prophets, who predict by virtue of their ignorance, may as well go on announcing the fall of theatre. Theatre will continue, as long as its expressive powers are enhanced, as long as it serves its era without submitting itself to technology. . . .[45]

The techniques were not new, but borrowed from cabaret entertainment, according to Franz Servaes, who had previously dubbed Piscator the "gravedigger of the theater," primarily because of his incorporation of film into theatrical stagings. What, he demanded, did the adaptation have to do with theatre:

> What does this have to do with drama and theatre? The enormous experience of the world war is pulled to the lower level of cabaret style satire and therefore robbed of all dignity. For the stimulation of the howling masses.[46]

Critics who came expecting conventional theatrical illusionism were indeed likely to be disappointed; Fritz Engel agreed with Servaes:

> Just experimentation without proper subject, without a goal to create a work of art from poetry and theatre, constantly puttering around and experimenting technically, isn't enough. In fact is nothing at all.[47]

As for the scenic means, he continued, "There's not a complete illusion."

Having checked his preconceptions at the door, Ernst Heilborn was prepared to accept the technical innovations. Grosz's drawings reminded him of the "chalk-talk," quick-sketch, artists in cabaret entertainment, only he found the effect delightful and much improved by the rapidity of film. The new form transcended its origins:

> And the quick chalk artist is no ordinary variety show character, but a genuine artist, who due to the rapidity of film, becomes a comic magician.[48]

Heilborn's analysis of the function of the film and its role in the new theatre, as illustration rather than illusion, was farsighted; he also realized that a new kind of illusion, which he called movement-illusion, was being substituted for conventional theatrical experience:

And this seems to me the essential: the stage here took on a totally new probability. The space has its own conventions, the movement has its own as well. Movement becomes independent of the space and has a different point of view.

This time a new importance was given to film. Besides the changing scenery, it provides the "illustration." George Grosz produced the boldly sketched presentation. Caricatures. But caricatures materializing and disappearing.

Not so different from the chalk artist in a variety program. A line here, a dot there. And suddenly those dots become a pair of eyes and then the lines climb around in a way that makes a face, now a whole figure appears—and suddenly everything vanishes and the artist starts a new game. One's attention is focused all the time. There are no dull moments in this "Theater."[49]

Even his old enemy Servaes admitted that Piscator's use of film was justified in this production: "In 'Schwejk' Piscator has assigned in general a more sensible role to the film."[50] He liked the caricatures by Grosz and even the moving sidewalks, though he chose to believe their comic effects were unintentional, and thought that all but Piscator's partisans would be perplexed by this performance.

Several critics praised Edmund Meisel's music, which smoothed the rapid changes of stage pictures. Emil Faktor wrote:

To the excitement of these [stage] realities were added irony and satire through animation and film sketches by hard-hitting political polemicist George Grosz. And Meisel's accompaniment maintains its distance in smooth collaboration.[51]

Meisel's music, which incorporated military marches and Czech hurdy-gurdy tunes, added local color. Meisel frequently wrote the music for Piscator productions. In 1928 he composed the score for the production of Brecht's *Mann ist Mann* at the Volksbühne, Berlin. Many years after the event, Wieland Herzfelde remembered the catalytic effect of the music in joining disparate temperaments: "More over, in the Schwejk production music played an essential role. It bridged the differences between Hasek and Grosz and even between Hasek and Piscator."[52] Meisel's credits also included the accompaniment to the first showings of Eisenstein's *Potemkin* and original compositions for Jessner's *Hamlet*.

Viennese accents were more frequently heard than those of Prague, commented several critics. In general Pallenberg overshadowed the other performers, regular members of Piscator's company. Anton Edthofer as Lukasch, "slim and noble," was frequently noticed by critics. Similarly Oskar Sima, who played the sheriff who apprehends Schwejk in the Budweiser Anabasis: "Oscar Sima tossed off a brilliant Sheriff. A great ox who drinks himself out of his mind."[53] Faktor, who praised Edthofer and Sima, was less pleased with other members of the cast:[54] "So grand a Schwejk wouldn't have suffered from a stronger cast. With notable exceptions, too much foil. . . ."[55]

Three scenes were consistently mentioned by critics: Schwejk's volunteering for service in which he was pushed in a wheelchair by Frau Müller, the scenes between Schwejk and the military doctor, and finally the Budweiser Anabasis for which Piscator combined lighting effects, titles, set pieces, and projections to give the illusion of movement. In general, these scenes, which must be considered the highpoints of the drama, were ones in which the maximum of new techniques was used. Two of them are scenes which depend heavily on movement.

The final word on *Schwejk* belongs not to the daily critics, some of whom were aware that the nature of theatre was undergoing a change before their eyes, but to Piscator who wrote: "The form which *Schwejk* assumed was certainly neither ideal nor final. As in the case of *Rasputin*, it was an embryonic dramatic form intended for the writers of future generations."[56]

7

Der Kandidat

A revival of Carl Sternheim's political comedy, *Der Kandidat*, opened in late January 1930 in the Kammerspiele of the Deutsches Theater. Hans Hinrich directed the production, which Grosz designed, and the cast included a rising young star of the German theatre, Peter Lorre. The show enjoyed a marginally successful run—for that time and theatre—of 41 performances, despite lukewarm reviews.

It was a precarious moment to revive a farce on political candidacy. Sternheim's play, a translation with slight modifications of Flaubert's *Le Candidat*, first performed with little success in Paris in 1874, had received its premiere in Vienna in 1915. It is a tribute to the play's universality or a telling comment on its essentially flaccid treatment of social issues, that the drama could retain relevancy in three such different societies: the French Third Republic, the Austro-Hungarian Empire, and the Weimar Republic in the grip of a severe economic crisis. The form is traditional, derived from Molière. *Der Kandidat* is an elegantly turned, cuckold farce in which the colliding self-interests of all the *dramatis personnae* provide a suspenseful gavotte toward the final sifting out of motives. The characters never quite modify their national identities; Sternheim's middle class Germans reveal their French antecedents. The basic thrust of the satire is directed at politicians' self-serving in a parliamentary state, although there are occasional jabs at the leftover aristocracy and more tolerant jibes at love's folly. Since the comedy is largely at the expense of the processes of a republic, the wellsprings of the drama appear conservative. Appearing at the onslaught of the world-wide economic depression, the ambivalent comedy could be interpreted in varying manners. Since no ideal is held up in contrast with the petty villainy and self-seeking of the players, the audience remains free to provide its own political solution to the inadequacies of the parliamentary system as portrayed in the drama. In a larger sense, Flaubert and Sternheim suggest that any form of government will be undermined by Human Nature's self-serving.

The Plot of *Der Kandidat*

The German adaptation follows the form of Flaubert's play in its division into four acts with scene notation by entrances. Sternheim found equivalents for the French surnames: Rousselin, the would-be candidate, becomes Russek, for instance. Settings included the exterior of his house, the interior, and a meeting hall across the street. Russek, a man for whom no sacrifice is too great for the privilege of having his card engraved, "M.d.R.," appears rather late in the first act, after several scenes have developed the circumstances of his political career.

Russek's candidacy and eventual election are achieved through a total lack of commitment to fixed principles. He is willing to entertain the possibility of the marriage of his daughter, Luise, to the young Count Achim, although he disapproves of the young man's not working. At the same time he accepts the liberal support of her real lover, Grübel, while he allows himself to be nominated by the conservative count. Similarly, he prefers not to realize the reasons for Bach's support. The latter, a young proletariat newspaper editor, covets Russek's wife. Another candidate, Seidenschnur, owes money to Russek, while Grübel, in turn, owes Seidenschnur.

In the restaurant-meeting hall scenes, before a crowd of voters, Russek is shown in a particularly bad light. Grübel almost saves the day for his future father-in-law by interpreting away his conservatism. Further negotiations go on with the old count, who wants to marry his son to Luise. Various businessmen arrive to remind Russek of what his election will cost him in favors. By the final moments of the play, when he learns of his election, the audience knows that Bach is carrying on with Frau Russek, and that Luise, tired of being bartered, is eloping with Grübel. Russek has won, at the cost of every vestige of integrity. The parallels for Grosz and his fellow opponents of the Republic with President Ebert, and other Weimar politicians, must have been killing.

Sternheim is rather faithful to Flaubert, and his principal modifications are structural changes in the final act. He makes clear that Luise is running off with her beloved. Flaubert leaves us in doubt. Sternheim also reduces an unwieldy plethora of servant-messengers. More is made in the French play of Seidenschnur's yielding when Russek forgives his debt. A single very important scene which lifts Flaubert's comedy out of the realm of conventional farce and gives it an allegorical twist is also deleted. In Flaubert's text (sc. 10), as Rousselin waits for the polls to close, a beggar blunders in through the open door. Rousselin at first tries to get rid of him, but finds he cannot adequately deal with the blindman:

Beggar: Charity, please. They say you're rich.
It's for a little bread. How weak I am!
Rousselin: (discouraged) I can't fight with a blind man![1]

He then gives the stranger his watch, finally to be rid of him. The beggar promises to pray for the candidate. Flaubert's scene is not without humor, but it also serves an important function in portraying Rousselin's inadequacy in human relations. In the final analysis it is this scene which makes Flaubert's comedy modern, and it is the omission of the incident which makes Sternheim's play a more tightly constructed and more superficial entertainment.

Grosz's Designs

The composition of flats into box settings determined the act breaks in Flaubert's play. Sternheim followed this scenic convention. Within these limitations Grosz designed three interesting settings for *Der Kandidat*. The play could have been given a less conventional staging, with the risk that critics would point out a disparity between conventional material and flamboyant staging. As it was, Jhering suggested that Grosz was not given freedom to caricature. Before commenting on Jhering's criticism it might be well to mention a few factors influencing Grosz's designs in 1930. The force of his political vituperation was falling off, and generally consisted of repetitions of earlier themes. Not unrelated to the infrequency of political caricature in this period was the growing preoccupation with the New Realism in Grosz's easel work. Grosz wrote an article, which was translated into French, in which he criticized the over-produced, escapist films with which the film industry sopped the appetites of the petty bourgeoisie, particularly their need to aspire to riches and magnificence. Throughout this article he calls for a focus on the ordinary, a realistic reference to everyday life rather than fantasy. The essay is relevant to his participation in the New Realism and also to the shape his political thought was assuming. He wrote:

I'd also like to see the next door room, not that room enriched by thought and grand intentions, built by well-known architects, but simply the room at hand, just as in ordinary life.[2]

Such insistence on the value of the prosaic, workaday world, is quite contrary to the imaginative historical treatment he himself had produced only a few years before for *Das trunkene Schiff.*

In *Das Kandidat* Grosz renounced a good opportunity for overstated, sumptuous interiors. Russek's house might well have elicited such treatment.

Grosz's emphasis is rather on workable ground plans and carefully selected detail, instantly recognizable for its economic and social connotations. In this show, and *Grischa* which followed, Grosz worked as an illustrator might, bringing alive a piece of fiction. He made numerous costume studies (Plates 38–39), but these are not ordinary costume sketches. They are also character sketches in which he examines certain physical attributes that a fictitious character might possess. His drawings suggest gesture and sometimes grouping. Caspar Neher is probably the best known example of an illustrator-designer. Neher's drawings influenced Brecht's blocking at the Berliner Ensemble; similarly Grosz's imaginative illustrations of characters and groupings bring to life the dramatic texts and may well have influenced the direction of the last two performances he designed in the Weimar Republic.

The unlikely proximity of the restaurant to Russek's elegant house and the cramped space in front of the house, make Grosz's setting for the first two acts (Plate 40) seem improbable, and therefore appropriately farcical, if slightly cramped. His ability to assemble convincing detail, such as the molding about Russek's door, the architecture of the restaurant, etc., convinces us, despite the obviously theatrical ground plan. Comic detail lightens the scene: the red striped awning of Russek's window and the lamb incorporated in the restaurant's sign, "Zum Lamm," the controlled patches of grass constituting Russek's front yard, even the shape of the tree silhouetted against a bright sky cyclorama.

The same juxtaposition of comic detail produces a more striking effect in the interior of the restaurant. The stage from which Russek addresses his audience is set with an idyllic landscape: the sort of snow scene with firs, frozen pond, setting sun, and snug house which might appeal to middle class taste. Grosz was having so much fun with the idea that he made a separate watercolor study of the cupid-decorated proscenium arch and landscape beyond. The overall setting might horrify the "professional" designer, for it combines ground plan and rendering by adopting a very high vantage. What Grosz intended is absolutely clear, but the setting on stage could not possibly have appeared to the audience as his sketch does. Grosz's observant eye captured the atmosphere of such places perfectly: plaster casts, pretentious detail in the stage and proscenium, juxtaposed with the prominent *Herren* and *Damen* rooms flanking the stage and the inelegant bulletin board with its lamp. Grosz was amused, but he was not exaggerating to the point of parody.

In order to capture the prosperous comfort of the Russek establishment, Grosz made several drawings of interiors. At first he made the mistake, noted in the case of the restaurant, of combining ground plan and rendering. In his most finished sketch, various elements which he had once considered were eventually rejected in this sketch: a fireplace, skylight, and rather odd partitions between entry hall and library. One critic spoke of Otto Wallburg's interpretation of Russek as "false Biedermann," and the same might be said for Grosz's mixture of modern furniture and interior architecture from an earlier but indefinite period. A wide window across the stage right, upstage wall permits Russek to watch for the results of the polls and to be surrounded by his admirers in the final tableau. Top hats were a symbol for Grosz of the artifice of political office. In various transformations of the room an umbrella-coat rack, accommodating several top hats, is a constant. In his sketch for the play's final moments, Grosz shows Russek in the interior gazing out at top hats raised on umbrella tips to the level of the window sill. An inscription by Grosz reads,"Hoh Russek."

Grosz imagined Russek as the jovial and prosperous burgher dressed in a double-breasted, well-tailored business suit. Frau Russek is the perfect middle class lady: a hand delicately raised to touch her pearls. Luise, flat-chested, dreamy, and something of a flapper, is a younger version of her mother. Miss Evelyn, the English companion, long-jawed, toothy, and dressed in a masculinizing double-breasted suit is a caricature of the English governess. The young count, Achim, is an ineffectual and shy fashion plate (Plate 39). The shabby respectability of the notary, Dettmichel, the Count's perpetual cat's paw in the marriage-candidacy game, is demonstrated in his badly fitting coat and vest. Like Dettmichel, Bach, the poet and Frau Russek's seducer, carries a portfolio (Plate 38). He wears knickers and a single-breasted coat with boutonnière. Lips pursed in inspired concentration, he scribbles as he walks. If other elements of society are caricatured, the working man is certainly less than idealized in Grosz's portrait of Hüther, whom Grübel brings to call on Russek. He looks slightly uncomfortable in his respectable suit, but the shape of his head suggests a Frankenstein figure, an impression his smile does little to dispel.

Critical Reaction

The strong statement contained in Grosz's costume-character sketches was not, apparently, instrumented on stage. Jhering, one of the few critics to mention specifically Grosz's designs, was troubled by the too-decorous style of the director, Hans Hinrich, and by the tameness, rather than the caricature in Grosz's work as it appeared in production. Whether the fault was Grosz's or Hinrich's, it is difficult to reconcile Jhering's remarks[3] with those of Fritz Engel, who thought the production accentuated the "drastic, quick-action, burlesque"[4] side of things.

Difficulties with the transposition of the play were twofold, as Jhering pointed out: French political tradition as well as French farce remained alien to German sensibilities. The stereotypical characters were not shared by the two societies:

> But it doesn't strike home. A common mistake. It is possible to write a political farce with typical characters and stock situations in France, a country with a strong political tradition. One simply transfers the comedy scheme with its cuckold and lover to the political machinery. In Germany one has to do a lot of preparation of conditions beforehand. Simple slogans won't do. No connections will be made. Mentioning party labels won't do. They go over our heads. Stereotypes won't do. Love tangles, corruption and the money business and profiteering won't do. Especially in those days, in prewar Germany, the audience had to be taught the political ABC's (corruption, personal power mania) first before it could understand the results.[5]

Of the names connected with this production, two are well-known today: Peter Lorre and George Grosz. Hinrich and Otto Wallburg, who played Russek, were members of the Reinhardt group and remained relatively little known, although Hinrich's wife, Maria, appeared frequently in productions at the Deutsches Theatre. Lorre played the young poet-editor Bach. He was then 26 himself. He had studied in Vienna, joined an improvisational group at 17 and then traveled the customary route to Berlin by way of provincial German theatres. He had already appeared in Brecht's and Weill's *Happy End* (1929) and was on the verge of international fame with his performance in Fritz Lang's film *M*. The year after *Der Kandidat* not only brought this film, but a controversial stage performance. Brecht defended Lorre's mannered performance as Gayly Gay in *Mann ist Mann*. What Brecht saw in his fragmentary and episodic style of acting, which critics thought inconsistent, was interruptions based on "Gesten," successive and even contradictory attitudes embodied in the same character. Perhaps when the contributions toward the nonrealistic but also nondeclamatory style of acting in modern German theatre are finally sorted out, performances like Lorre's Bach as well as Steckel's pawnbroker in *Nebeneinander* will be seen to be pathfinding.

The critics considered Lorre as an actor somewhat apart from the rest of the production, but they applauded his efforts here. Jhering,[6] in particular, praised his search for a style appropriate to Sternheim's literature. Arthur Eloesser remarked on the interest of his character and the way he remained on the periphery.[7] Max Hochdorf praised the portrayal of the "fishy individual."[8]

In general critics were sympathetic to the actors' efforts to play unrealistic roles.[9] Jhering thought Wallburg something of a heavyweight in the role of the candidate. Eloesser commented on Wallburg's improvement as he dropped the more mechanically farcical style in the final scenes.

Hochdorf thought Wallburg went beyond Sternheim's meagre text in his creative performance.

Director and designer, Hinrich and Grosz, faded into the minor paragraphs of most reviews. Emphasis was on seeking a playing style adequate to the literary, farcical style of the text. His reasonable attack on the candidate displayed Grosz's talents bridled. Although reviewers might expect vitriol, Grosz's art was decidedly moving in another direction by the late twenties.

8

Der Streit um den Sergeanten Grischa

Arnold Zweig's *Der Streit um den Sergeanten Grischa* is singular among war stories for several reasons: above all, in embodying its antimilitaristic thesis in an intellectual and psychological probing of justice, rather than in horror-provoking description of combat, as *Die Wandlung* and, to a lesser extent, *Schwejk*, had done. Zweig's story concerns the fate of the Russian sergeant Grischa: sentenced to death unjustly, defended by the old Prussian, General von Lychow, Grischa is eventually executed in order to satisfy the autocratic Major-General Schieffenzahn. The beauty of Zweig's construction is that the battle for justice—and its eventual defeat—are presented in intellectual format, through the argument of the paternal General with his ruthless superior, and in emotional terms by the psychological portrait of Grischa, whose desire for life is sapped by the long process during which his fate hangs in the balance.

Grischa is also remarkable for the date when it was conceived and written, and for the manner in which it shifted between novel and dramatic form. Although conceived in 1917, Grischa was first written in 1921 as a play. The novel appeared in 1927, three years before the play and almost 30 years before the play was published.

Two plays which Grosz designed—*Grischa* and *Die Wandlung*—are outside the sphere of comedy, although both had comic moments and strong irony that might be considered comic. Zweig adapted what he originally called a "tragedy" as a novel. An RKO "All Talking" Film was then adapted from the novel and released in the United States in March 1930. Chester Morris starred in the American version. German critics were thoroughly familiar with the best-selling book, but not the film, when they saw the drama at its premiere in 1930 at the Theater am Nollendorfplatz, as a guest performance of the Deutsches Theater. Alexis Granowsky directed the production, which was designed by George Grosz and Piscator's staff designer, Traugott Müller.

Reaching a large circulation, the novel, the centerpiece of a trilogy, became, like Remarque's *All Quiet on the Western Front*, a *cause* among intellectuals, who saw the duplication and also simple continuation of the flaws of the *ancien régime* in the Weimar Republic. In the intervals between publication of the novel (1927) and publication of the play (1956), the author, a frequent contributor to *Die Weltbühne*, had moved with measured tread to the Left: this movement would culminate in his being chosen Minister of Culture of the East German State. His progress in the embrace of the Soviet Revolution is readily discernible in the revisions of the novel made evident by comparison with the play, particularly in insertions predicated on hindsight concerning the coming Russian Revolution. Zweig's grasp of social conditions somewhat redeems the artistic failure of his novel. Three themes recur: the position of the Jew in German society, as portrayed in the lawyer Posnanski and his secretary Bertin, and the increasing conflict between old aristocratic families, such as von Lychow's, and the new urban interests, such as Schieffenzahn and von Brettschneider, are central to the action. A third theme, the growing sense of political identity of the workers, was usually commented upon by other groups, rather than being structurally integrated in the novel.

A dramatization would seem, perforce, to remove some of the most specious stylistic devices of the novel, such as comparison of Grischa's situation with that of a wild lynx, a parallel in which Zweig attributed human consciousness to the lynx. While such questionable comparisons in forced manner were purged, important minor characters were also. Accentuated in the dramatic form was Grischa's romantic involvement with the strange refugee from war's disruptions, Babka, who, while trying to protect him on his Eastern journey, gives Grischa the fatal, false identification papers of the dead Bjuschew. Babka eventually bears Grischa's posthumous child. Reviewers, in general admirers of the novel, complained of two effects which staging had wrought: an accentuation of sentimentality, particularly in scenes between Grischa and Babka, and an exaggeration of moral polarities in the characterization of the military: von Lychow vs. Schieffenzahn. Herbert Jhering's summation may not be completely just to Zweig; his points, however, voice the opinion of several critics in a slightly more vociferous and articulate form:

> Arnold Zweig was the first to treat the war theme visibly for the German and European public. But this should not keep us from stating that Arnold Zweig, the writer, who has to emphasize sentimentality because he lacks emotion from within, always fights the poet, who intends to stimulate and intellectually clarify feeling through literary interpretation. Arnold Zweig is clever and sentimental. But he is not intellectual and emotionally powerful.[1]

Paul Fechter echoed a charge of sentimentality and formlessness:

> For this sequence of scenes is no play. It is a drawn-out, broad report which lacks the lung power for its length. Arnold Zweig's energy is sufficient for small, calm sentimental

scenes; when he wants to show the battle of powers, it turns into harsh, primitive and asthmatic theatre.[2]

Synopsis

At the headquarters in Brest-Litowsk (I, i) the Commander of the Eastern Front, Major-General Schieffenzahn, ruminates on means to control defections and spying with his subordinate, Brettschneider. Schieffenzahn dictates a memo:

> To avoid spreading unrest, the following order stands: All deserters from beyond our lines must identify themselves as such and report to the nearest post commander within twenty-four hours. Anyone hanging around our positions must be brought before the closest court martial and shot as a spy.[3]

In the following scene one luckless victim of this proclamation begins his escape into the snowy night. As guards patrol the barbed wire enclosing a German prison camp, Grischa and his compatriot Aljoscha, who is staying behind, say their farewells. In counterpoint to Grischa's homesickness the guards discuss the coming revolution. This snowy night gives way to a clear day, and Grischa is discovered with several companions gathered about a campfire (I, iii, Plate 41). This band of refugees includes Babka, whose family has been destroyed during the early years of the War. She becomes Grischa's mate. On the Eastern front, a telegraph office (I, iv) receives Schieffenzahn's command concerning the immediate execution of deserters and foreign intruders caught behind German lines. Briefly the band of outlaws discusses Grischa's departure from the group, his homeward journey (I, v). In Babka's hideaway Grischa makes love to the strange, prematurely-aged girl. Not realizing the consequences of her protective act, she gives her new friend the clothes of her former lover, Bjuschew, who is now dead. Along with these she relays instructions about his new identity, an escape route, and contacts along the way. At the beginning of the second act, two watchmen, conversing quietly, move along a village street, while Grischa narrowly escapes due to their inattention. In the warm waiting room of the regimental prison at Merwinsk (II, ii) Grischa soon sits, however, with his captors. The friendly, even boisterous, interchange between Grischa and his captors is interrupted by a party of officers: Lt. Winfried, Lawyer Posnanski, Sergeant Spierauge. To this delegation, Grischa repeats lies about his identity. Following the newly received order, Posnanski charges Grischa with spying. At Winfried's execution order, Grischa is convulsed with fright. He then collapses with laughter screaming, "the devil with Bjuschew!" and asserts his real identity.

Zweig's stage directions frequently call for polyscenic setting, a scenic form which was managed by use of the Nollendorfplatz Theater's revolving stage, as in the third scene of the second act. Center stage is Posnanski's room where the clerk Bertin and Lt. Winfried are desperately trying to verify Grischa's identity; to either side of this cube run wires to other telephone boards. As miles of telephone wires are supposed to be down, Bertin's anxious messages are garbled; the replies he receives are unrelated to his questions. His fate still undetermined, Grischa is assigned a keeper, Sacht, who is instructed to allow the Russian a measure of freedom while the inquiry continues (II, iv). In the next scene (II, v) two of Grischa's former captors at the detention camp hold a friendly reunion with their former prisoner and establish before Posnanski that Grischa is Paprotkin rather than Bjuschew. The Commander of the post, Lychow (Plate 42), visits Posnanski's office (Plate 43) and detects in Grischa, beneath the tattered uniform, a handsome specimen who might well serve as orderly. As the second act curtain descends, Grischa's salvation seems unofficially assured.

In the courtyard of the prison (III, i), Babka joins Grischa, who appears content with his new form of captivity. He explains proudly to her the complications of his case, symbolized by the thick sheaf of correspondence between military lawyers. Homesickness for Russia, his wife, and child, is at first the sole motive for his impatience with imprisonment. Then Babka tells him she is pregnant and thus adds another cause for his discontent.

Meanwhile (III, ii), the powers against Grischa begin to coalesce. Schieffenzahn decides to oppose forcefully Lychow's objections: an example is needed to maintain discipline. The garden party (III, iii) which follows is actually an account of several encounters at separate locales during the celebration at Lychow's country estate-headquarters. The focus, achieved by use of the revolve, accompanies the news of Schieffenzahn's tough stand as it passes through the ranks and up to Lychow. Grischa is innocently and blissfully drunk on what has been given him as he serves, enjoying the most marvelous party he has ever attended, and unaware of the reversal of his own fate. In the Garden Pavilion, Posnanski shows the latest dispatch to Winfried, who decides to go directly to his uncle, the General. A few moments later Lychow is assuring Grischa that his case is going well, when into the happy group around the paternal Lychow and the tipsy Russian servant, comes Winfried with his bad news. Now the focus changes as the General crosses the stage. He confronts Posnanski concerning the legality of Schieffenzahn's orders. The old Prussian is undeterred by arguments of political expediency. As the revolve turns once more, a group of officers and medical personnel are brought down center and Grischa exchanges cordial good nights with the General.

Passing a tense night on duty, two telephone operators discuss Lychow's chances in Grischa's case. They reiterate the absurdity of the situation (IV, i). In the prison courtyard (IV, ii) Babka tries to convince Grischa to flee, but he answers her entreaties with resignation. Winfried and his sweetheart, the nurse Barbe, talk with von Lychow in the garden of Winfried's house (IV, iii) as the General prepares for his confrontation with Schieffenzahn. At Brest-Litowsk (IV, iv) the meeting at last takes place in Schieffenzahn's office. Arguing situational morality, Schieffenzahn opposes the Prussian's rigid sense of right and wrong: "Your Excellency, we are at war. War is made from human lives. The one who wins is right, the one who loses is wrong."[4]

Lychow rejoins that such flagrant abuse of justice can only have a demoralizing effect—rather than inspiring discipline—on the troops. His political philosophy is based on the principle that the State embodies justice rather than merely dispensing it. In the face of Schieffenzahn's obstinate table-thumping, Lychow maintains his idealism. Finally he announces that only one course remains to him: direct appeal to the Kaiser. The problem is time, for Grischa is condemned that night, unless a reprieve or retraction is granted.

The fifth act begins with a series of short scenes of anxious waiting: Babka gathers fruit by moonlight and muses on a life continually disrupted by violence (V, i). At the telephone switchboard, two operators and an orderly wait as Bertin enters to inquire about the news (V, ii); in Winfried's room, a group including several nurses sits anxiously hoping for a reprieve (V, iii). The vigil continues in Grischa's cell (V, iv), as Babka and Sacht join the prisoner in a drink. Winfried comes to offer Grischa a means of escape, but he refuses. Resignation achieved, he does not want to hope again. Winfried tries to assume responsibility for freeing Grischa but his subordinate, Corporal Sacht, with regret, refuses to allow it.

Spierauge and von Brettschneider give last minute instructions to the eight men of the firing squad. In the prison waiting room (V, vi) standing before Spierauge and some of the garrison, Grischa dictates a verbal testament disposing of his money and few possessions. The execution squad arrives. Grischa disappears to the sound of drumbeats steadily increasing in volume and culminating in the rifles' detonations. What is almost an epilogue is depicted in the scene which follows at the post canteen (V, viii). When soldiers register their reaction to the execution, Lychow is proven right: Grischa's execution has demoralized rather than heightened respect for authority. Zweig introduced a second epilogue to the play, one not found in the novel. Months later, Sophie, the aristocratic nurse and her lover, Bertin, the Jewish author, walk through the cemetery at Merwinsk searching for Grischa's plot. Coming to place a lock of Grischa's child's hair on the grave, Babka carries her child and pauses to discuss her return to Russia, to a new society promising greater hope for her child.

Critical Reaction

Alexis Granowsky, founder and leader of the Moscow Jewish Theater, which performed the plays of Scholom Aleichem, had toured his company in Western Europe only a year before he directed the production of Zweig's *Grischa*. Rather than return to the Soviet Union, Granowsky remained in Europe as a film and stage director. Even those critics with severe reservations mentioned the public acclaim accorded Granowsky, Zweig, and the performers. Considering this popularity, it is strange that the production was presented no more than 30 times. The rambling script, enriched by a few highly dramatic moments (critics were agreed in choosing Grischa's first reprieve, the garden party, the Lychow-Schieffenzahn interview, and Winfried's final attempt to free Grischa as the dramatic highpoints) lasted some three and one half hours in performance, a long evening in any theatre.

Berlin critics' standards for directing during this period of "director's theatre," were extremely sophisticated. Granowsky was inevitably compared, to his detriment, with Reinhardt and Piscator. In fact, since he was working in Piscator's former theatre, with two of Piscator's scenographers, he could scarcely escape comparison with the Communist director.[5] It was somewhat unjust to blame the canteen epilogue on Granowsky as if he, rather than Zweig, had attempted to imitate Piscator's passion for historical context. Particularly for the garden party scene, Granowsky was ranked with Reinhardt, generally acknowleged master of the use of the revolve. The odd vantage of Berlin critics seems to have blinded them to Granowsky's lack of exposure to the directors the critics knew best; surely Meyerhold would have provided a similar and more direct influence than Piscator on the Russian director. Berlin critics had seen the Jewish Theater on tour, and there was controversy about the degree to which Granowsky had curtailed the customarily heavy stylization of this group. Certainly his German actors, the general mounting of the performance and setting, suggest realistic standards for the acting style. The selective realism and distanced observation of *Neue Sachlichkeit* were instrumented in the careful attention to economic, political, and social traits of characters: an echo of Zweig's own practice. Granowsky was working, however, with a rather hybrid form, balancing the objectivity of Grosz's and Müller's settings against the extremely poetic and sentimental undertow in Zweig's writing. Selective realism in *Grischa*—real objects placed on a bare stage, with little attempt at total illusionism—is not too distant from the scenic formula which Brecht and Neher were developing for Brecht's plays. But stylization heightened by realism, rather than vice versa, could easily become diffuse. Jhering was the most severe in his judgment of the director: "He had reached dead end with his stylisation and turned to the opposite: the formless play of the senses. Particularly the staging is without any form."[6] But was such formlessness really the director's fault? There was certainly room for doubt, and critics such as Paul Fechter thought that Granowsky was skillfully covering the play's essential weaknesses by his method. Karol Rathaus's music was not mentioned by reviewers.

Performers

Two performers, not surprisingly the heroes of the play, drew unanimous praise from critics: Friedrich Kayssler, who played General von Lychow, and Hermann Thimig, who was the unfortunate Russian sergeant. Jhering called Thimig, "modest, economical and coherent, also splendid." Kurt Pinthus was even more unguarded in his praise:

> Hermann Thimig was Grischa; at first with that fresh, versatile simplicity he is recognized for—however, as he was slowly being worn down and before his death, he developed a calm and later a magnificent spirituality never before seen from this actor, penetrating him as well as us.[7]

Arthur Eloesser thought the highlight of this fine performance was Grischa's nearly mute farewell to Babka, Winfried, and Sacht. Hermann Thimig, member of a respected Austrian theatre family, was almost 40 years old when he impersonated Grischa. He had played young heroes in the Meiningen theatre and then came to Berlin, where he was typed in comic roles at the Deutsches Theater. Critics repeatedly noted that in *Grischa* he had outgrown such light-hearted endeavors. Friedrich Kayssler, in his mid-50s, was not much older than Thimig—not nearly as much older than Thimig, as in the Lychow-Grischa relationship. Kayssler had been associated with Reinhardt since the first *Schall und Rauch*. He enjoyed his greatest success in *The Prince of Homburg* and had played the title role in *Peer Gynt*. Kurt Pinthus wrote: "The Officer played by Kayssler is wonderful. Despite the murderous nonsense around him, he is content with himself and the world and therefore wishes to straighten out the world by means of the Grischa case."[8]

It was, of course, easier to admire performances of two appealing characters, such as Grischa and Lychow, than to respond to the more difficult roles, such as Schieffenzahn; a figure not unlike the villains of nineteenth-century melodramas. Critics were quick to note that Hermann Vallentin's caricature of a repressive autocrat was a recognizable portrait of General von Ludendorff. Babka, played by Dagny Servaes, was an even more difficult part than Schieffenzahn. The character is scarcely convincing in Zweig's fleshed-out novel. Fritz Engel wrote, "All Dagny Servaes' fine acting abilities are inspired by the wildwoman Babka."[9] While Jhering thought her "too weak," Eloesser thought a German director might better have guided the actress in a difficult part: "Under the command of a German director, Dagny Servaes' part would probably have been broader, heavier and more distinctly Russian."[10]

Three others of the cast[11] received particular mention for the excellence of their performance: Max Landa, who played Posnanski, Günther Hadank in the role of the adjutant, Winfried, and Ernst Ginsberg as Bertin.

Settings and Costumes

The nature of Grosz's collaboration with Traugott Müller, as in the case of his cooperative endeavors with Heartfield and Suhr, remains mysterious. We may only guess from the nearly complete catalog of costume designs and the numerous sketches for settings that Grosz did copious designs which were then constructed under Müller's watchful eye.

Traugott Müller's masterful use of machinery certainly qualified him as a professional scenographer. His productions designed for Piscator included *Gewitter über Gottland, Hoppla wir leben!* and *Rasputin.* His work was strongly experimental, particularly in the use of materials rarely seen then on stage.

Wolfgang Storch, quoting Eloesser, compares Grosz's designs for *Grischa* with bright toys and suggests that they demonstrate a lightly ironical Expressionism and New Objectivity.[12] The apparent contradiction contains more truth than it appears at first: Grosz's caricatures of the army staff do seem to be achieved within a basically Expressionist idiom, while his settings show a strong mark of observed reality and an acceptance of "things"— particularly furnishings—which is characteristic of New Objectivism. The hallmark of isolated, carefully chosen objects is stronger than in his designs for Kaiser, and closer to the realism of *Der Kandidat.* There, however, the realistic settings gave a more complete illusion: here furnishings were placed on the stage with little attempt to relate them to an overall stage picture, although in relation with one another they formed habitats which were frequently psychological portraits of given characters.

As in *Der Kandidat,* for both settings and costumes, Grosz appears to have worked as an illustrator might, from the novel rather than from the play and its brief stage directions. We can only speculate also on what Zweig's verbal instructions to his scenographer might have been. Grosz provided a valuable service for his foreign director, Granowsky: a firsthand knowledge of characteristic military types (dating not only from his own war experiences but from childhood when his mother had managed an officers' club in Stolp). His illustrational notations might also have been useful in blocking and gestures. In this respect, Grosz's work in *Grischa,* as in *Der Kandidat,* bears comparison with Neher's habit of suggesting the blocking of actual scenes, as Grosz's "illustration" of the outlaw band (Plate 41) may have in *Grischa*. Grosz followed, of course, the standard uniforms of the military figures in his rogues' gallery; an important contribution was visual interpretation of these Germanic types to Granowsky and providing sketches for the makeup of many characters.

Grosz succeeded in making several settings outgrowths of specific characters: a sort of psychological portraiture for which he was gifted and which was related to the use of cumulative detail in his satirical drawings discussed in Chapter 1. One of Grosz's psychological portraits was the design for Posnanski's office: two sketches of this curious habitat, a retreat from the war, survive. The more finished drawing is in Köln, but the vital elements are already assembled in the Estate sketch (Plate 43). The lawyer Posnanski and his scribe, Bertin, are Jewish.

While there are many hints in the novel concerning the psychology of the two men, it was left to Grosz to exercise his imagination in choosing objects to furnish the office where they were supposed to work. Posnanski is a cultivated Berlin lawyer; his aesthetic appreciation was made clear in the novel by his learned admiration for an intricate plaster ceiling, here by a plaster cast of Venus. Bertin is the most radical of the Germans in the novel: his Jewish identity and his profession as an author suggest that he is an alter ego for Zweig. Grosz's method was to assemble various real—but sometimes improbable—objects, such as a classical Venus, the iron stove, a Japanese screen, rolltop desk, framed collection of butterflies, typing desk, etc. Psychologically significant items are placed, with careful attention to the rich colors which create a cozy atmosphere, in interesting relationships.

At times this apparent love of the familiar, the furnishings and taste of the middle class, approaches *kitsch* and led Grosz into the danger of being *nondramatic*. Paul Fechter characterized the curious mixture of the recognizable, sentimental, and bitter, a combination that was effective for engaging the audience in the world of the play. "But Granowsky's lyrical softness matches Zweig's sentimentality pretty well. George Grosz, the designer, omitted all harshness and came up with a colorful naturalness, as with real birch furniture and the neatly painted walls of the fort, everything came nicely together and created a friendly bourgeois atmosphere pleasing to the audience."[13] But not all the designs were as successful as the one for Posnanski's room or Grosz's detailed attempt to counterfeit the Russian architecture of the house at Merwinsk. Jhering confessed his puzzlement about the contributions of the two scenographers:

> George Grosz' contribution to this performance will always be a mystery to me. (I assume he did the nice offices and the telephone dispatchers'). Less in doubt, is the contribution by Traugott Müller: the styleless mix of decorative junk, something he once claimed to have gotten rid of.[14]

The simplest method was to blame the stage on Traugott Müller. The critic for *Welt am Abend* wrote: "Traugott Müller's scene designs were of a ridiculous primitiveness that ought not be discussed."[15] Lack of illusionism similarly struck several of the reviewers as naiveté: the demand for a convincing illusionism, particularly in staging melodrama, was still prevalent. While the "Brechtian" stage, with its synthetic assemblage of real objects, is familiar to us all today, we have also come to expect such décors to accompany a certain kind of play, far removed from the sentimental, realistic melodrama in *Grischa*.

9

The Happiest Man in America?

Grosz first visited the United States in 1931, and in January 1932 made his move permanent. Unlike many of his Berlin colleagues, he did not view his stay in the United States as exile. Grosz tried to champion his adopted home. He made terrific efforts to adapt and to be positive. During the later years of the thirties, his theatrical associates often sought refuge in the United States. Brecht left Germany for Scandinavia, then came to the West Coast. Piscator made a film in the Soviet Union and eventually arrived in New York. Heartfield went to Prague, then to the Soviet Union, and finally to Great Britain. Mehring, Viertel, Aufricht, Toller, Herzfelde, and Huelsenbeck all came to America. Grosz was in touch with these and many other refugees. With those like Heartfield, Brecht, and Piscator who remained faithful to their Marxist views, political opinion appears to have separated Grosz from his former collaborators.

A letter to Piscator explains why *Schwejk* could not be successfully performed in the United States.[1] Another apologizes to Piscator for a "barroom brawl" in Grosz's living room in 1939.[2] Grosz could not resist jibes at Stalin as a self-appointed deity. And he was increasingly doubtful about any art that served doctrine. Early letters[3] to "Bertie" Brecht concerning illustrations—those for "Three Soldiers"—and ones projected for Brecht's dramatic works, sound genuinely enthusiastic. Grosz admired his colleague and probably had a good idea of his importance long before the world knew. There is a falling-off, however, and by 1946 when Grosz was opening a large exhibition, and Charles Laughton and Brecht were in New York for the upcoming production of *Galileo*, Grosz reported to Hermann Borchardt that he was photographed with both theatre artists, then with Laughton, as Brecht was not well enough known. His American optimism did not extend to the production of *Galileo*.[4] Peter Grosz assures me that Grosz saw Brecht no more when they both returned to Berlin in the fifties.[5]

In another early and important letter,[6] Grosz addresses the President of Universal Pictures Corp., Carl Laemmle. Just a year after his immigration, Grosz sent his theatre sketches—which he cautions are working drawings rather than finished renderings—to Laemmle. He was, at this time, full of ideas about films, and he mentions to Laemmle that he has been interested in film since its inception (true, if one recalls Pierre in St. Nazaire). In his autobiography, with customary self-amusement and fine attention to the nuances of polite cruelty, in the chapter called "The Story of Devilbiss Spray,"[7] Grosz narrated an employment interview with a Hollywood movie tycoon. Newly arrived and supporting himself by teaching, he recalled that he had done some scene painting and that set design might now supplement his income, especially if he could design for Hollywood. The producer's summary brush-off surprised and disappointed Grosz. Thus the autobiography dismissed his post-Dada theatrical activity in a single anecdote. The autobiography does not mention that many of the plays he designed were valuable dramatic works. Grosz's belief—and he joked himself of his faith in the legend that Hollywood's streets were paved with gold—that he might succeed in American film is indicative of his relative naiveté about the American entertainment industry. In his letter[8] to Piscator in 1935, he appears, however, to realize clearly how difficult the situation for any "Leftist" theatre artist; how great the power of producing organizations such as the Theater Guild and the need for total success on Broadway; and the absence of smaller and less commercial enterprises. Of his Berlin colleagues, those who made a career in American theatre and film, Kurt Weill and Peter Lorre, for instance, did so by adapting their standards to the American market.

Grosz had moved from Dadaism, Constructivism, and the New Objectivity to another brand of realism in his American period. He painted the dunes on Cape Cod and nudes a little reminiscent of Rubens. In the United States he earned much of his living from illustration for magazines like *Esquire*. This, as well as his rejection of political art and satire, had a great influence on his style. His pessimism emerged in stick figures, survivors who wandered in the void or personified the after-product of great loss. The figures represented a very genuine and painful emotional reality, but they were not attractive and they remain undervalued today.

Grosz once replied to an interviewer's question, "Where is paradise," with "In America." By and large he chose not to see the social disorder and chaos of post-Depression American streets. He chose to be bereft of proximate antagonists for his satire. He ignored young American artists who were actually his heirs, if not disciples, such as Ben Shahn and Jack Levine. Although he experienced considerable success with commissions, and illustrations, and showed frequently, his public was often disappointed by the placidity of his American paintings. New York painting was becoming increasingly abstract; Grosz may have felt more on the periphery than he would have liked. After frequent invitations Grosz finally accepted an offer to return to Germany in 1953. He played the role of the American tourist to the hilt. Teaching possibilities and a return to the theatre both seemed impending.

Nearly a quarter of a century had elapsed between the last of Grosz's designs in the Weimar Republic's Berlin and his return to the divided Berlin of 1954. The production which brought Grosz back was part of the Berliner Festwochen that also included Thornton Wilder's *The Matchmaker*, directed by Tyrone Guthrie, and the Viennese Chamber Theater's performance of Büchner's *Leonce and Lena*. Nostalgia for the artistic ferment of the twenties almost obscured the originality of the German premiere of an evening of American ballets, designed mostly with good-natured wit, by George Grosz. *Ballet Ballads*, as they were called on Broadway or *Bilderbogen aus Amerika* as they were dubbed in Berlin, was a variety of homespun *Gesamtkunstwerk:* tales told by combining song and dance, which American reviewers had classed as an important step in the development of the American musical theatre. One group sang the story as another set danced the action. The form superficially recalled the Brecht-Weill-Balanchine collaboration on *The Seven Deadly Sins*, performed in Paris more than two decades before *Ballet Ballads* was written. Contributing to the nostalgia of German critics was a vague knowledge of Grosz's once important role in Berlin theatre and the fame of Ernst Josef Aufricht, the producer. It was he who first presented the *Threepenny Opera* in 1928 at the Theater am Schiffbauerdamm (now the home base for the Berliner Ensemble), which he managed after the collapse of Die Truppe. Aufricht, a founding member with Piscator of Die Truppe, even played that unpleasant gentleman who had recognized his fur coat in the garderobe of the nightclub and thus precipitated the pawnbroker's tragedy in *Nebeneinander*, designed by Grosz in 1923. The return of two of the Weimar Republic's culture heroes could only excite the press. Grosz was eager for publicity, as his letter to Aufricht shows.

Although he had not even been born when Grosz, Heartfield, Piscator, Neher, and Brecht had been creating innovative theatrical forms in the twenties, Egon Monk, the young translator and director of *Bilderbogen*, had been assistant to Brecht at the Berliner Ensemble and was thus strongly associated with Epic Theatre in the critics' minds. No wonder that when Wiet Palar danced Cocaine Lil, one reviewer could only think back to the twenties for a reference and came up with Josephine Baker! Combating this curious sentimentality for the bad old days, Grosz appeared rather vulgar in his newspaper interviews. He was quoted or misquoted as saying that beer was not so good as before the war, that his famous friends included Faulkner, Laughton, etc., and that his time was worth $250 per half-hour in New York.

Bilderbogen had premiered in New York six years before the German performance. The first presentation was held at the Maxine Elliot Theatre on May 9, 1949, under the auspices of the Experimental Theatre Company. The original production was such a success that it moved to the Music Box where the run, of nine weeks, was shaky. Jerome Moross, the composer of

Frankie and Johnny and the opera *The Golden Apple*, collaborated with John Latouche, who was also the librettist for this opera and for *The Ballad of Baby Doe*. The initial bill of this new lyric theatre consisted of three one-act dance-operas: "Susannah and the Elder" with choreography by Katherine Litz; "Willie the Weeper" choreographed by Paul Godkin; and "The Eccentricities of Davy Crockett," choreographed by Hanya Holm. The Aufricht production substituted a tale, "Red Riding Hood '54" for Crockett's adventures, which had generally been considered the most successful of the three initial sketches by American reviewers. Still another revival and grouping of the four operas occurred in New York in 1961; this time "Davy Crockett" and "Willy the Weeper" were juxtaposed with "Red Riding Hood."

Grosz wrote to Aufricht in July 1954, sending two sketches for a painted curtain and one costume sketch.[9] The Walter Bornemann scene shop was already scheduled to execute the settings. These sketches have disappeared and only costume drawings for *Bilderbogen* remained in the Estate collection. In addition, Grosz is not credited by reviewers with design of the settings; some substitution must have been made for Ekkehard Grübler received good reviews for his simple suggestive settings.

Synopsis

The opening tale of the Berlin program was an unusual interpretation of the Biblical story of Susannah and the Elders.[10] Jens Keith-did the choreography. Moross and Latouche transposed the events of the story to a revival meeting in the American Bible Belt. As the pastor told the story, his congregation, which was also the costumed chorus, joined in, and the action was acted out by various frontier types. Thus when the Elders, Moe and Joe, decked out in spirit gum beards (blue and orange ones to suit Grosz's fantasy) spied on the bathing Susannah, it was from between symbolic branches held by two dancers. The mock-sinister beards were donned in view of the audience, and the dirty old men were essentially a comic duo throughout. The tale closed with a moral:

> Now as ye sow ye all shall reap
> And virtue's made of heavenly stuff
> And beauty is only skin deep—
> For the Elders that was deep enough!

The center piece of the Berlin trilogy was the story of Willie (Plate 44), whose dreams are induced by marijuana. If Grosz's gift for prophetic involvement in social issues seems uncanny, the addict theme had appeared in his work as early as 1916. The authors of "Willie the Weeper" left one area of rural American folklore to peruse the urban folk scene. The musical idiom

changed from hymns to jazz. Willie was portrayed in a variety of moods—
lonely, famous, baffled, and self-sufficient as the drug induced fantasies:
Willie as millionaire, jazz saxophonist-king, gangster-hero, and sheriff.
Inevitably his self-sufficiency is doomed by the seductive Cocaine Lil. When
Willie imagined himself as a tycoon, he sang:

> Buy a railroad in Greece and a rice field in Java,
> Then by bomber to Fujiyama to monopolize the lava ...
> Buy some cotton in Spain and then spin it in Egypt
> Sell it later in Decatur where citizens can be gypped.
>
> . . . .
> His record may be checkered
> But it's really superb;
> He took bus'ness from the gutter
> And raised it to the curb. . . .

Willie as saxophonist was similarly an unsavory fantasy figure:

> In Turkestan, In Kansas City, Kan.
> In Moxie or Biloxi, who's the favorite man?
> Who gets the Dukes as well as the Jukes as well as the Kallikaks?
> It's twelve-tone Willie with his sexy sax.[11]

To Cocaine Lil, he sang, "Give me a little love while my hands are still warm,
I crave affection in a not too simple form. . . . " And his willing seduction was
generally agreed to be one of the most effective moments of the three ballets,
no matter which of the successive Lils, Sono Osato (1948), Wiet Palar
(1954), or Carmen de Lavallade (1961) performed the sultry dance.[12]

The final number of the Berlin evening[13] was a reworking of the Little
Red Riding Hood story for adults. Little wonder that the Berlin critics
thought this sketch with its cheap irony belonged in a cabaret. The updated
version began with a spring bacchanal presided over by a bawdy Mother
Nature. Members of the chorus were costumed as trees. A Good-Humor
man wooed a teen-aged Red Riding Hood. Then she was pursued by an
aging Viennese wolf. At the sight of an eight-carat diamond, however, Red
Riding Hood reverses roles. She goes home to chuck her grandmother out of
bed, the better to seduce the Wolf. In order to avoid the impression that this
encounter should be taken seriously, as a comment on the newly divulged
Kinsey Report, the Berlin program stressed its subtitle: "Eine Silly-
Symphonie, ein Hinweis auf die Walt-Disney Filme."

Critical Reaction

On the whole, the Broadway "Cocktail am Darstellung Wort und Musik,"
did not intoxicate the Berlin critics. It had been a mistake to tout the evening

as a new form of theatre; critics realized both the Brecht-Weill origins and the simple debt to cabaret. Walter Kaul's assessment of the "new" genre was a typical one:

> The ballet ballads are—as the name ballad already indicates—species of the "epic theatre" which was proclaimed here during the twenties and is now gaining ground in the United States. If these ballet ballads did not display such pretentious style, one could simply say they were cabaret sketches.[14]

The Netherlandish dancer Wiet Palar captured the reviewers' hearts; they liked Egon Monk's direction, but not his translation, and the musical direction by Martin Mülzer of the two pianists and singers was considered excellent. Curiously the critics' grimaces over the parody of Red Riding Hood did not reflect the general public's reaction:

> The audience accepted the attempts to make Broadway musical experiments palatable to the Berlin audience, but it appreciated—according to the applause—only the modern Red Riding Hood devouring the lascivious wolf.[15]

Reactions were evenly divided as to whether "Susannah" or "Willie" was the best of the three, and which was the most American of all.

The décors, simple suggestive settings by a rising young designer, Ekkehard Grübler, were applauded. Grosz's costumes drew a mixed reaction. Perhaps the strongest criticism came from Walter Kaul: ". . . while George Grosz' costumes seemed alien to the theatre."[16]

Who would ever have thought there could be a relationship between Grandma Moses and George Grosz, but Dora Fehling saw one in subject matter at least: ". . . George Grosz' costumes stayed close to the floral imagery of Musaus fairy tales and the naive motifs of that famous American painting grandmother."[17]

Grosz's fame as a vicious satirist made the designs seem tame: the *Darmstädter Echo's* reaction was a typical one: "George Grosz, once the most poignant satirist in the world, created the costumes: not at all aggressive but pretty and gay."[18]

Reviewers' complaints that Grosz no longer used his customary, beloved bitterness in designing probably pleased the artist more than those critics who saw his designs as duplication of the motifs (particularly in "Willie the Weeper") of the twenties. The reviewers who complained of his new serenity supported his case that he had outgrown satire, that he had changed, he was not caught in the web of nostalgia surrounding the production nor was Grosz trapped in the sentimental admiration for the good old bad times.

Not since his sketches for Shaw had Grosz so thoroughly concentrated on diversionary humor, lightly mocking the identity of his characters but attacking neither the dramatis personae nor the audience. Avoiding confrontation with his audience, and hence the risk of offending the spectators, may indeed have lessened the effect of his costumes. They still had wit, but the humor was more playful and less angry than in previous designs. Grosz was freed, too, from the preoccupation with reference to observed reality that had challenged him in settings for Kaiser's plays, *Grischa* and *Der Kandidat*. The new freedom, and the less aggressive humor, resulted in designs which are simple, dramatic and perhaps the most Expressionistic of Grosz's career. The basis for all his costumes were dance tights. Wit came out in juxtaposition of materials: the herringbone of the Wolf's pants, for instance, beautifully echoed the texture of his bushy tail (Plate 45). There was understatement: Red Riding Hood is conventional in order that her role may be the funnier when reversed. Grosz's gift for exaggerating symbol (recall his designs with such details as the editor's whistle in *Androcles*, the top hat of Herr Rat in *Kanzlist Krehler*) could be even more pronounced in costumes for a nonrealistic ballet, and so red gloves and an enormous red gun in a shoulder holster came to symbolize the gangster. When Grosz became more dramatic, his vision veered from comedy to the grotesque, as in the chorus for "Willie": patches of flesh-colored tights show through the jagged tatters of bloodied costumes. Heads are replaced by masses of exposed brain. The effect is of a psychotic vision induced by drug, and resembles the stick figures of Grosz's own late apocalyptic visions. Willie as the Saxophonist (Plate 44) came closest to Grosz's former portrayal of menacing evil: the gold derby, white coat with its appliqués of gold saxophones, and Willie's small Hitler moustache, add up to a sinister effect. American reviewers experienced difficulties in distinguishing Willie's fantasies, but Grosz's costumes provided a clear guide to the Berlin spectators in differentiating one role from another.

The watercolor style of the sketches was symptomatic of a new freedom: in no set of drawings for the Berlin theatre in the twenties was Grosz so thoroughly at ease. He had consciously studied commercial illustrators' techniques during his protracted American sojourn. The artful lack of finish in the sketches for costumes and his command of a loose watercolor technique demonstrate the impact of his admiration for manual dexterity on his earlier, more tightly-controlled style. Frequently, without the necessary exposure to a body of work, critics have been harsh in their judgments of Grosz's American period and rejected such facility as trite or empty. In fact, the freedom of technique was closely wed to the more Expressionist approach and the less directly satirical, less castigating humor.

The paradox of the artist's choice of a basically Expressionist idiom to portray characters with whom he had little emotional involvement is explained in part by the nature of the ballets themselves, in part by his own painting at the time. In *Caesar and Cleopatra* and *Androcles*, where Grosz had also sought diversionary humor, the change in tone was largely attributable to his anglophilia. In the case of *Bilderbogen aus Amerika*, his pro-American stance must account for much of his reticence to attack American society, even in sequences such as "Willie" which provided a good opportunity. During the years immediately prior to his return to Berlin, Grosz had survived the era in which the House Un-American Activities Committee attempted to intimidate former Communists. Under these circumstances his genuine gratitude toward the United States might also have combined with an understandable self-censorship. In articles and drawings he partially recanted, or at least clarified, his former position.[19]

The results of this beneficent humor and lack of desire to flay his adopted country are likely, in this final example of his theatrical work, to appear as mere cleverness. Diversionary humor is traditional, not conducive to innovative techniques of staging; castigating humor served Grosz and his collaborators as a springboard to the use of new and exciting techniques during the Weimar Republic. By the fifties, there was no longer a fight for justice, no more anger with authority, and only a hint of moralizing. Grosz's earlier work could almost be defined by what was absent in these, his last theatrical drawings.

Plate 1. "The war did me a lot of good, like a spa."
Lithograph (from the projections for *Schwejk*)
from the portfolio *Hintergrund*, 26 × 17 cm., 1928.

Plate 2. Agamemnon puppet design, *Orestie*
Ink and watercolor, 49 × 37.5 cm., 1919.

Plate 3. Aegisthus puppet design, *Orestie*
   Ink and watercolor, 49 × 37.5 cm., 1919.

Plate 4. Courtyard, *Caesar and Cleopatra*.
Ink and watercolor, 36 × 43 cm., 1920.

Plate 5. Costume for a Roman soldier, *Caesar and Cleopatra*
Watercolor, 14¼ × 10½", 1920.

Plate 6. Apollodorus, *Caesar and Cleopatra.*
Sepia ink and watercolor, 48.5 × 32 cm., 1920.

Plate 7. Caesar, costume sketch, *Caesar and Cleopatra.*
Pencil, watercolor and gold paint, 36 × 26.5 cm., 1920.

Plate 8. Captain, costume sketch, *Androcles and the Lion.*
Ink and watercolor, 48.5 × 23 cm., 1924.

Plate 9. Referee (Editor), *Androcles and the Lion.*
Ink and watercolor, 47.5 × 35 cm., 1924.

Plate 10. Ida and the Student, *Methusalem*.
Ink and watercolor, 41 × 53 cm., 1922.

Methusalem's living room, *Methusalem*
(The Odol Design).
Ink and watercolor, 15½ × 20¼″, 1922.

Plate 12.   Methuselah (sic) *Methusalem.*
            Watercolor, bronze paint, pen and ink, 20¾ × 16¼″, 1922.
            Collection, The Museum of Modern Art, New York,
            Mr. and Mrs. Werner E. Josten.

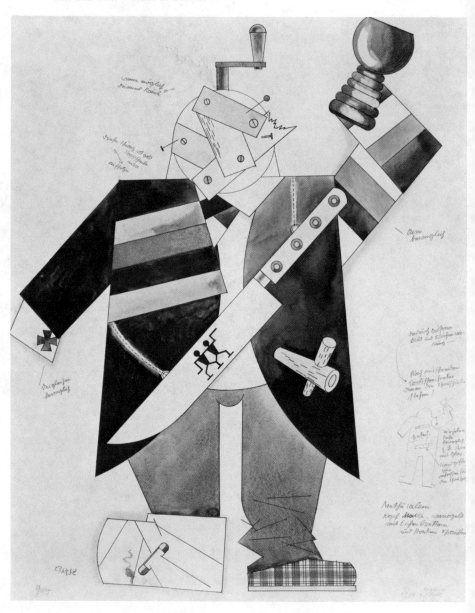

Plate 13. Amalia, *Methusalem.*
Ink and watercolor, 1922.

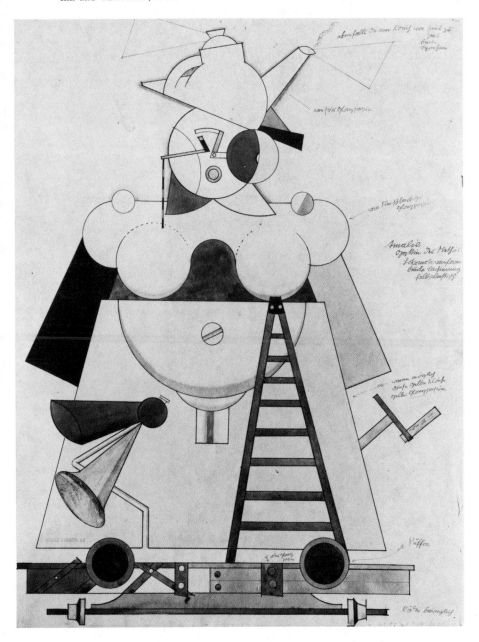

Plate 14.   The Student, *Methusalem.*
Watercolor, 20½ × 14½″, 1922.
Contemporary Collection of the Cleveland Museum of Art.

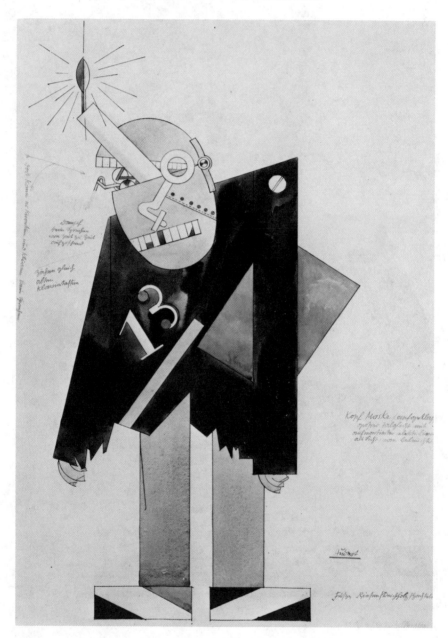

Plate 15. Frau Krehler costume design, *Kanzlist Krehler.*
Pencil, 40 × 24 cm., 1922.

Plate 16.   Krehler, costume design, *Kanzlist Krehler.*
Pencil, 40.5 × 19.5 irregular, 1922.

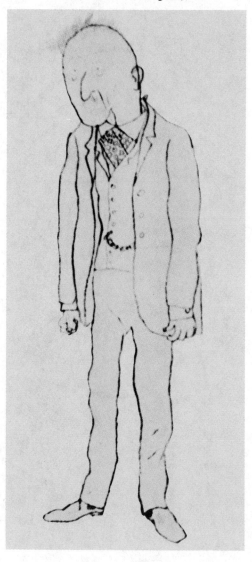

Plate 17. Night club setting, *Nebeneinander.*
Ink, watercolor, 37 ×50 cm., 1923.

Plate 18. Hallway, Pension Elvira, *Nebeneinander*. Watercolor, 36.5 × 50 cm., 1923.

Plate 19. Borsig's sister, costume sketch, *Nebeneinander*.
Ink and watercolor, 46 × 29.5 cm., 1923.

Plate 20. Prologue, *Wandlung.*
Ink, 35.5 × 46 cm., 1926.

Plate 21. Friedrich's house, *Wandlung*.
Pencil, watercolor, ink, 50.5 × 65 cm., 1926.

Plate 22. Café (Latin Quarter), projection, *Das trunkene Schiff*.
Ink, 12 3/8 × 25½, 1926.
Collection of The Museum of Modern Art, New York,
acquired through the Lillie P. Bliss Bequest.

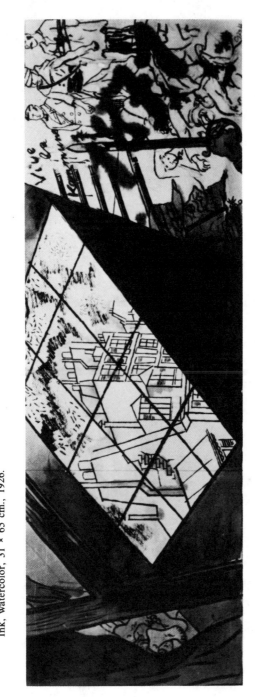

Plate 23. Verlaine's garret room, projection, *Das trunkene Schiff*. Ink, watercolor, 31 × 65 cm., 1926.

Plate 24. Prison at Mons, projection, *Das trunkene Schiff*.
Ink, watercolor, 52.5 × 65 cm., 1926.

Plate 25. Cyprus, projection, *Das trunkene Schiff*.
Ink and watercolor, 25 × 65 cm., 1926.

Plate 26. Farmyard, projection, *Das trunkene Schiff*.
Ink and watercolor, 20.9 × 30.6 cm., 1926.

Plate 27. Officer reading newspaper,
Two-dimensional cutout, *Schwejk.*
Watercolor, 50 × 39.5 cm., 1927.

Plate 28. Butcher reading newspaper,
          Two-dimensional cutout, *Schwejk*.
          Watercolor, 50 × 39.5 cm., 1927.

Plate 29. Worker reading newspaper,
Two-dimensional cutout, *Schwejk*.
Watercolor, 50 × 39.5 cm., 1927.

Plate 30. I Love You,
Lithograph (from the projections for *Schwejk*),
Plate 5 from the portfolio *Hintergrund*, 17 × 26 cm., 1927.

Plate 31. The Entire Population is a Bunch of Malingerers
Lithograph (from the projections for *Schwejk*),
Plate 6 from the portfolio *Hintergrund*, 17 × 26 cm., 1927.

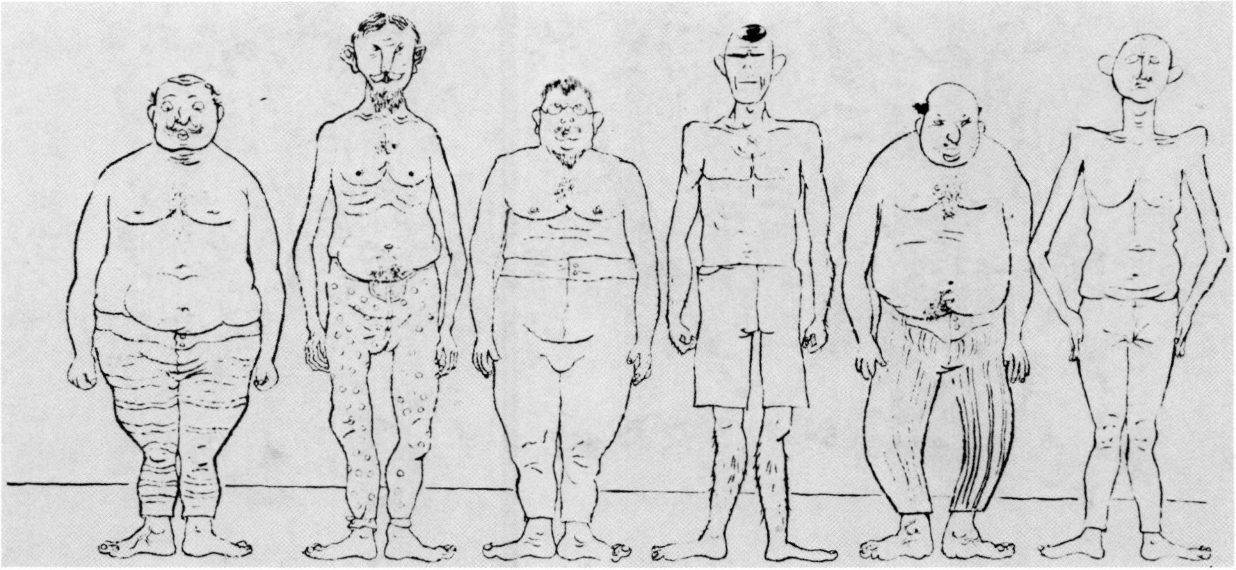

Plate 32. In Three Days You'll be Fit for Field Duty.
Lithograph (from the projections for *Schwejk*),
Plate 7 from the portfolio *Hintergrund*, 17 × 26 cm., 1927.

Plate 33. The Last Resort for Those Who Didn't Want to Fight was the Detention Barracks (title projection), *Schwejk*. Ink, 42 × 65 cm., 1927.

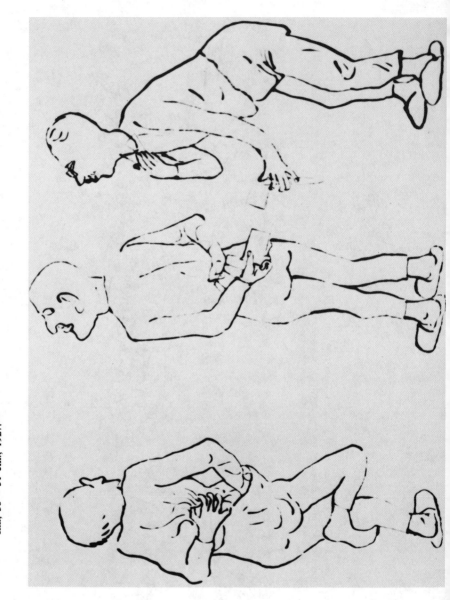

Plate 34. Three Cutout Figures from the Chaplain's Sermon, *Schwejk*. Ink, 38 × 51 cm., 1927.

Plate 35. Tree of Life, from the projections for *Schwejk*.
Plate 4, from the portfolio *Hintergrund*, 17 × 26 cm., 1927.

Plate 36. March to the Gallows and Transformation of Jailers to Dogs, *Schwejk*. Ink, 52.4 × 65 cm., 1927.

Plate 37. Beg to Report Sir, I am an Idiot, *Schwejk*.
Plate 1 from portfolio *Hintergrund,*
Lithograph, 26 × 17 cm., 1927.

Plate 38. Bach, costume design from *Der Kandidat*.
Pencil, 60 × 46 cm., 1930.

Plate 39. The Young Count Rheydt, costume design
from *Der Kandidat.*
Pencil, 60 × 46 cm., 1930.

Plate 40. Russek's house and Zum Lamm, setting for Act 1, *Der Kandidat*. Watercolor and ink, 47.8 × 66.5 cm., 1930.

Plate 41. The Outlaws, *Grischa*.
Watercolor and ink, 27½ × 20½ cm., 1930.

Plate 42.   von Lychow and Captain, costume design, *Grischa*.
60 × 46.5 cm., 1930.

Plate 43. Posnanski's office, *Grischa*.
46 × 66 cm., 1930.

Plate 44. Willie the Weeper as saxophonist, *Bilderbogen aus Amerika*. Watercolor, 40.6 × 27.2 cm., 1954.

Plate 45. Wolf, from Little Red Riding Hood,
          Bilderbogen aus Amerika.
          Watercolor, 42 × 29.5 cm., 1954.

Notes

Preface

1. *Orestie einfach klassisch*, December 9, 1919; *Cäser und Kleopatra*, December 22, 1920; *Kanzlist Krehler*, February 14, 1922; *Nebeneinander*, November 3, 1923; *Androkles und der Löwe*, February 2, 1924; *Das trunkene Schiff*, May 24, 1926; *Die Abenteuer des braven Soldat Schwejk*, January 23, 1928; *Der Kandidat*, January 23, 1930; *Der Streit am den Sergeanten Grischa*, March 31, 1930.

2. *Wandlung*, which he began for Piscator, and *Methusalem*, for which he planned costumes and settings in 1922. The *Methusalem* production in Berlin in 1924 did not use his designs.

3. *Bilderbogen aus Amerika*, September 22, 1954.

4. *Die Deutsche Theater Ausstellung*, Magdeburg, 1927. (Magdeburg, 1928) p. 218.

5. W. R. Fuerst and S. J. Hume, *Twentieth Century Stage Decoration*. (New York, 1929) 2 vols.

6. Léon Moussinac, *Tendances nouvelles de théâtre*. (Paris, 1931).

7. Oskar Fischel, *Das moderne Bühnenbild*. (Berlin, 1923).

8. Julius Bab, *Das Theater der Gegenwart*. (Leipzig, 1928).

9. Hans Rothe's *Blätter für die Reinhardt Bühne 1930/31* omits the designs for Piscator's unstaged revival of *Die Wandlung*. The chronology was written prior to the productions of *Grischa* and *Bilderbogen aus Amerika*. *Die Wandlung* is also omitted from Wolfgang Storch's chronology in Henning Rischbieter's *Bühne und bildende Kunst in XX. Jahrhundert* (Hannover, 1968). The English translation and edition of this book, *Art and Stage* (New York, 1969) adds the production of *Bilderbogen aus Amerika*, which the German edition omits. Storch gives the erroneous impression that the 1924 *Methusalem* employed Grosz's designs. *Friedrich's Theater-lexicon*, also edited by Henning Rischbieter, misdates the *Caesar and Cleopatra* production and repeats the error about *Methusalem*. Franz-josef Janssen's *Buhnenbildes in Deutschland* (Innaug. diss. Munich, 1957) does not give an explicit chronology, but within his text Janssen gives the impression that *Caesar* followed *Methusalem*, *Nebeneinander*, and *Der Kandidat*, p. 123. My own chronology is given in the unpub. diss. *The Theatrical Designs of George Grosz* (Yale Univ., 1970). Beth Lewis follows this in *George Grosz: Art and Politics in the Weimar Republic*. Herbert Knust and Hedy Landman appear to agree in the exhibition catalog for the Busch Reisinger three years later.

10. Michael Patterson, *The Revolution in German Theatre 1900-1933*. (Boston, 1981) pp. 188-203.

11. Catalog of designs related to each production follow the discussion of the production in my dissertation, which is available from University Microfilms. Size, media, and annotations are given where possible, along with the location at the time of the dissertation, 1970.

Chapter 1

1. The translation of Grosz's poem is from Sinclair Dombrow, "The German 'Babbit' on Stage," *Vanity Fair*, XX, 5 (1923) p. 96.

2. George Grosz, *A Little Yes and a Big No.* (New York, 1946).

3. Ibid., p. 27.

4. Ruth Berenson and Norbert Muhlen, "The Two Worlds of George Grosz," *George Grosz.* Bittner, ed. (New York, 1962) pp. 22, 26, 28.

5. Walter Mehring, *The Lost Library, Autobiography of a Culture.* (London, 1951), p. 147.

6. Siegfried Kracauer, *From Caligari to Hitler.* (Princeton, 1947), p. 19.

7. Erwin Piscator, *The Political Theatre* Hugh Rorrison, trans. (New York, 1978), pp. 39–40. Piscator's book was originally published in 1929 and was translated into several languages, but not English. In 1963 a new and revised German edition appeared, which forms the basis for this translation.

8. Ibid., pp. 265–66.

9. If we accept Ortega's dictum that the generation is the "hinge of history" then we must also put up with the arbitrariness of his method. In the case of Grosz and his era, I believe that the distinction can be a rewarding one. The experience dividing generations was definitely service in the First World War and reaction to that service. A study of birthdates of the principals in this essay yields two distinct generations: that of Reinhardt, born after 1870, too late to experience the Franco Prussian War, and that of Grosz, born after 1890. The younger generation would have been approximately 14 to 28 at the outbreak of World War I; that is, still young enough to serve in combat. A more complete listing of birthdates includes: Max Reinhardt, 1873-1943; Harry Kessler, 1868-1937; Siegfried Jacobsohn, 1881-1926; Alfred Kerr, 1867-1948; Herbert Ihering, 1888-1977; Erwin Piscator, 1893-1959; John Heartfield, 1891-1968; Alexis Granowsky, 1890-1937, Bert Brecht, 1898-1956; Ernst Toller, 1893-1939; George Grosz, 1893-1959.

10. Ernst Toller, *I was a German.* (New York, 1930) p. 99.

11. Wieland Herzfelde in a letter to Andrew DeShong, August 9, 1969 (translated).

12. Richard O'Boyer, "Profiles," *The New Yorker*, (Dec. 4, 1943), p. 39.

13. Harry Kessler, "In the Twenties," Sarah Gainam, transl. *Encounter*, (July, 1967), XXIX, 1, p. 3.

14. Peter Gay, *Weimar Culture.* (New York, 1968), p. 70.

15. H. F. Garten, *Modern German Drama.* (New York, 1962), p. 175.

16. Berenson and Muhlen, *The Two Worlds*, p. 28.

17. George Grosz, *George Grosz.* Herbert Bittner, ed. (London, 1965), p. 32.

18. W. H. Auden, "Notes on the Comic," *The Dyer's Hand.* (New York, 1962), p. 385.

19. E. H. Gombrich, *Art and Illusion.* (Princeton, 1969), pp. 330-58.

Chapter 2

1. The composite description of Grosz's studio is assembled from his interviews with Richard O'Boyer, "Profiles," *The New Yorker*, (Nov. 27,1943), pp. 32–36, 38; Dec. 4, 1943, pp. 39–44; Dec. 11, 1943, pp. 37–42, 44; and George Grosz, *A Little Yes and a Big No.* (New York, 1946), and Walter Mehring, *Berlin Dada.* (Zurich, 1957).

2. Marcel Janco, quoted in *Dada: Monograph of a Movement*, Willy Verkauf, ed. (New York, 1961), p. 28.

3. Richard Huelsenbeck, *Dada Almanach*, p. 105.

4. Hans Richter, "Dada as Movement," in *Dada: Monograph of a Movement*, Willy Verkauf, ed., p. 64.

5. Performances of the Club Dada included: 12 April, 1918: "Neue sezession," Berlin; June, 1918 "Cafe Austria"; April 30, 1919: Graphic Gallery J. B. Neumann; May 24, 1919: Meister Saal, Berlin; 7 and 13 Dec., 1919, Die Tribune, Charlottenburg; Jan. 1920: Performances in Dresden and Leipzig; March, 1920: in Teplitz-Schönau and two performances in Prague. The list is taken from Raoul Hausmann's account in Dada: Dokumente einer Bewegung (Catalog of the exhibition held Sept. 5–Oct. 19, 1958 at the Kunstverein für die Rheinlande und Westfalen, Düsseldorf Kunsthalle.) (Düsseldorf, 1958) u.p.

6. Walter Mehring, *The Lost Library*, p. 152.

7. Richard O'Boyer, "Profiles," *The New Yorker*, (Dec. 4, 1943).

8. Henri Behar, *Étude sur le théâtre dada et surréaliste.* (Paris, 1967), p.15.

9. Tristan Tzara, quoted in Peter Schifferli, *Als Dada begann.* (Zurich, 1957), p. 56.

10. Alexis, "Besuch im Cabaret Dada," *Dada Almanach*, Richard Huelsenbeck, ed. (New York, 1966) pp. 135–41.

11. Quoted in Henning Rischbieter, *Bühne und bildende Kunst im XX. Jahrhundert.* (Hannover, 1968), p. 164.

12. Walter Mehring, *Berlin Dada.* (Zurich, 1959), pp. 50–51.

13. Quoted in Günther Rühle, *Theater für die Republik.* (Frankfurt, 1967), p. 175.

14. Walter Mehring, *Das neue Ketzerbrevier* (Kölh, 1962), p. 23 (translated).

15. Ibid., p. 21 (translated).

16. Quoted in Rudolf Hosch, *Kabarett von gestern.* (Berlin, 1967), p. 195 (translated).

17. Grosz, *A Little Yes*, pp. 165–66.

18. Hösch, *Kabarett*, p. 196 (translated).

19. Friedrich Holländer, *Von Kopf bis Fuss.* (Munich, 1965), pp. 100–101.

20. Rosemarie Hammer made reconstructions of some of the puppets, presumably using documents in the collection of John Heartfield's widow. These puppets are not reproduced but are catalogued in John Heartfield, Ausstellung der Deutschen Akademie der Kunste, Uwe Schneede, ed. (Berlin, 1969). The exhibition was held in Stuttgart concurrently with one of Grosz's works.

21. Fritz Windisch, "Schall und Rauch, *Freiheit*, (Dec. 9, 1919), p. 2.

22. A. Z., "Schall und Rauch," *Vorwärts* (Dec. 9, 1919), p. 2.

23. J. W. B., "Schall und Rauch," *Berliner Tageblatt*, (Dec. 9, 1919), p. 3.

24. Erwin Piscator, *Das Politische Theater*. (Berlin, 1929; Hamburg, 1963), p. 190.

Chapter 3

1. Henning Rischbieter, *Bühne und bildende Kunst im XX. Jahrhundert*. (Hannover, 1968), p. 172

2. For a discussion of the cinematic vogue for historical pageantry in which social and economic causation were replaced by psychological studies of historic personalities, see Siegfried Kracauer, *From Caligari to Hitler*. (Princeton, 1947), p. 52.

3. Edward Gordon Craig, *Towards a New Theatre*. (London, 1913), p. 51.

4. Franzjosef Janssen, *Bühnenbild und bildende Kunstler: Ein Beitrag zur Geschichte des modernen Bühnenbildes in Deutschland*. (Inaugural Diss., Munich, 1957) pp. 124–25 (translated).

5. Wieland Herzfelde in a letter to Andrew DeShong, Aug. 9, 1969 (translated).

6. The cast included: Rufio: Wilhelm Diegelmann; Pothinus: Edgard Klitsch; Theodotus: Hugo Döblin; Achillas: Ludwig Körner; Charmian: Ilsabe Dieck; and Iras: Edith Merten.

7. Herbert Jhering, *Von Reinhardt bis Brecht*. (Berlin, 1961) I, p. 174 (translated).

8. Max Hochdorf, *Vorwärts*, Dec. 23, 1920, p. 2 (translated).

9. Paul Wiegler, *Die Dame*, XLVIII, 9, pp. 11–12 (translated).

10. G. B. Shaw, *Complete Plays with Prefaces*. (New York, 1963), V, p. 476.

11. Ibid., V, p. 472.

12. Wieland Herzfelde, *John Heartfield*. (Leipzig, 1962), Plate 78.

13. Julius Bab, "III. The Theater in the German Language Area Since World War," in *The Theater in a Changing Europe*, Thomas H. Dickinson, ed. (New York, 1937), p. 128.

14. The cast included: Lion: Rudolf Maass; Emperor: Berthold Rose; Ferrovius: Raul Lange; Centurio: Carl Kahlmann; and Maegara: Alice Torning.

15. A. M., "Androkles und der Löwe," *Vossische Zeitung*, (Feb. 5, 1924), p. 2.

Chapter 4

1. Iwan Goll—Claire Goll Briefe (Berlin, 1966), p. 46 (translated).

2. This is a thorny issue. Sinclair Dombrow's article "The German 'Babbit' on Stage," (*Vanity Fair*, July, 1923) is the only source contemporary with the production I have found indicating that Grosz's designs were used. The date of the article shows that the production was still in the planning stage. Dombrow refers to the production, ". . . now being presented in Berlin," p. 65. Later accounts that describe the play as having been performed with Grosz's costumes include those by H. Rischbieter, John I. H. Baur, Martin Esslin and the editors of the French edition of Goll's play. Gösta Bergman states that Grosz's designs were used: *den Moderna Teaterns Genombrott 1890–1925*, p. 489. On the other hand, Hans Rothe in the Journal of the Reinhardt Stage states clearly that the intended designs were not employed. (*Blätter der Reinhardt Bühnen*, Heft V, Spielzeit, 1929/30, p. 1.)

3. Iwan Goll, "Methusalem or the Eternal Bourgeois," translated by Clinton J. Atkinson and Arthur S. Wensinger, *Plays for a New Theater.* (New York, 1966), p. 100.

4. Ibid., p. 68.

5. Ibid., p. 75.

6. Ibid., p. 81.

7. Ibid., p. 93.

8. Ibid., p. 58.

9. Goll quoted in Richard West, "George Grosz: Figure for Iwan Goll's Methusalem," *The Bulletin of the Cleveland Museum of Art,* (April, 1968), p. 93.

10. Michel Corvin, "Georges Ribemont Dessaignes et le laboratoire 'Art et Action', *Cahiers Dada-Surréalisme,* (I, 1966), pp. 164–65 (translated).

Chapter 5

1. Georg Kaiser, *Kanzlist Krehler.* (Potsdam, 1922), p. 14 (translated).

2. Paul Weiglin, Kammerspiele des Deutschen Theaters, "*Unterhaltungsbeilage der Täglichen Rundschau,* (Feb. 15, 1922), p. 95.

3. Felix Stössinger, *Freiheit,* (Feb. 15, 1922), p. 2.

4. Herbert Jhering, *Von Reinhardt bis Brecht,* p. 249.

5. Ibid., pp. 334–337.

6. Max Hochdorf, "Fassadendramatik, " *Vorwärts,* (Nov. 5, 1923), p. 2.

7. Monty Jacobs, "Georg Kaisers Volkstück," *Vossiche Zeitung,* (Nov. 5, 1923), p. 2.

8. The cast included: Pawnbroker: Leonard Steckel; Daughter: Erna Schöller; Luise: Greta Schröder; Neumann: Rudolf Forster; Lock Inspector: Karl Hannemann; His Wife: Mea Steuermann; Franz Krüger: Ernst Martens; Borsig: Erhard Siedel; His Sister: Lyda Salmonova; Kracht: Martin Wolfgang; Elsasser: Fritz Lion; Police Commissioner: Aribert Wäscher; Pension Mgr: Frigga Braut; First Woman: Lotte Fliess; Second Woman: Sidonia Lorm; First Man: Ernst Josef Auffricht; Hat Check Lady: Hedy Schlichter; Lady: Eve Seeberg; Pastor: Sigismund von Radecki; Director: Hans Karl Georg; Porter: Sven Holm; boy: Carl Heinz Carell; Chambermaid: Ilse Bachmann; Orderly: Hans Schalla; and Policeman: Will Nowakowski.

9. Siegfried Jacobsohn, quoted in Günther Rühle, *Theater für die Republik,* (Frankfurt, 1967), p. 485.

10. Ibid., p. 485 (translated).

11. George Kenworthy, *Georg Kaiser.* (Oxford, 1957), p. 65.

12. Hans Roselieb, *Frankfurter Zeitung,* (Nov. 10, 1923), p. 1.

Chapter 6

1. *George Grosz Ausstellung,* Akademie der Kunste, (Berlin, 1962) u.p.

2. Ibid.

3. Erwin Piscator. *The Political Theater.* Hugh Rorrison, trans. from the 1963 German edition. (New York, 1978) pp. 39–40.

4. Ibid., p. 23

5. Ibid. p. 22.

6. Ernst Toller, "Transfiguration," Edward Crankshaw, trans. in *Seven Plays* (New York, 1936), p. 106.

7. Piscator, *Political Theater*, p. 119.

8. Erwin Piscator, "Zu meiner Inszenierung von Zech'Das trunkene Schiff' in der Berliner Volksbühne", *Das Kunstblatt*, (July, 1926), pp. 274–75 (translated).

9. Ibid., pp. 273–74 (translated).

10. Ibid., p. 275 (translated).

11. Ibid., p. 275 (translated).

12. Ibid. (translated).

13. Alfred Klaar, *Vossische Zeitung*, (May 23, 1926), p. 10.

14. Alfred Kerr, *Berliner Tageblatt*, (May 22, 1926) p. 2.

15. Otto Steinicke, "Das trunkene Schiff," *Feuilleton der Roten Fahne.* (May, 1926), p. 1.

16. Ernst Degner, "Ein Bühnen Bilderbogen," *Vorwärts,* (May 22, 1926), p. 2.

17. Ernst Heilborn, "Berliner Theater," *Frankfurter Zeitung,* (May 27, 1926), p. 1 (translated).

18. The cast included: Grete Bäck, Ellen Widmann, Ilse Baerwald, Franze Roloff, Therese Thieszen, Julius Schmidt, Reusz, Manz, Nunberg and Ferdinand Asback in the role of Hassan, Rimbaud's native man.

19. Degner, *Ein Bühnen Bilderbogen* (translated).

20. Heilborn, *Berliner Theater* (translated).

21. Klaar, *Vassische Zeitung* (translated).

22. Steinicke, *Das trunkene Schiff* (translated).

23. Piscator, *Political Theater*, p. 254.

24. Pavel Petr, *Hasek's "Schwejk" in Deutschland.* (Berlin, 1963), p. 101.

25. Ibid.

26. Ibid., p. 103 (translated).

27. Petr, *Hasek's Schwejk*, p. 105.

28. Translation of the stage directions by Mordecai Gorelik, *New Theatres for Old.* (New York, 1962), p. 385.

29. Piscator, *Political Theatre*, p. 261.

30. Ibid.

31. Jaroslav Hasek, *The Good Soldier Schwejk*, Paul Selver, trans. (New York, 1930), p. 352.

32. Gorelik, *New Theatres*, p. 386.

33. Piscator, *Political Theater,* p. 267.

34. Gasbarra quoted in Piscator, *Political Theater,* p. 259.

35. Piscator, *Political Theater,* p. 265.

36. George Grosz, in Piscator, *Political Theater,* pp. 266–67.

37. Piscator, *Political Theater,* p. 193.

38. Ibid., p. 303.

39. Piscator, *Political Theater.* p. 261.

40. Ibid., p. 268.

41. Petr. *Hasek's Schwejk,* p. 104.

42. Servaes in Gunther Ruhle, *Theater für die Republik.* (Frankfurt, 1967), p. 847.

43. Kert Kersten quoted in Piscator, *Political Theatre,* p. 269.

44. Oskar Schlemmer, *Letters and Diaries of Oskar Schlemmer,* (Middletown, 1972), p. 226.

45. Jacobs quoted in Ruhle, *Theater für die Republik,* p. 845 (translated).

46. Servaes quoted in Rühle, *Theatre für die Republik,* pp. 848 (translated).

47. Fritz Engel, *Berliner Tageblatt* (January 24, 1928), p. 4 (translated).

48. Ernst Heilborn, *Frankfurter Zeitung,* (January 26, 1928), p. 3 (translated).

49. Ibid. (translated).

50. Servaes quoted in Rühle, *Theater für die Republik* p. 847 (translated).

51. Faktor quoted in *Theater für die Republik,* p. 843 (translated).

52. Wieland Herzfelde in a letter to Andrew DeShong, Sept. 8, 1969 (translated).

53. Faktor quoted in Rühle, *Theater für die Republik,* p. 843 (translated).

54. The cast also included: Elizabeth Neumann, Josef Danegger, Max Schreck, Hugo Werner-Kahle, Jano Furth, Prockle and Szakall.

55. Faktor quoted in Ruhle, *Theater für die Republik,* p. 844 (translated).

56. Piscator, *Political Theater,* p. 263.

Chapter 7

1. Gustave Flaubert, *Oeuvres complètes, XIV Théâtre.* (Paris, 1910), p. 153 (translated).

2. George Grosz, "Le Grand Monde, *La Révue du Cinéma,* (April 1, 1931), p. 15 (translated).

3. Herbert Jhering, *Von Reinhardt bis Brecht,* III, p. 44.

4. Fritz Engel, "Sternheim: 'Der Kandidat', *Berliner Tageblatt,* (January 28, 1930), p. 4.

5. Jhering, *Von Reinhardt bis Brecht,* p. 43 (translated).

6. Ibid., p. 44.

7. Arthur Eloesser, "Der Kandidat," *Vossische Zeitung,* (Jan. 29, 1930), p. 7.

8. Max Hochdorf, "'Der Kandidat' von Sternheim," *Vorwärts,* (Jan. 28, 1930), p. 3.

9. The cast included: Paul Horbiger: the Count; Toni van Eyck: Luise; Otto Wallburg:

Russek; Peter Lorre: Bach; among the other performers Maria Fein, Willi Forst, Wilhelm Bendow, Deepe, Paulmöller, Günther, and Lvovsky Schröder.

Chapter 8

1. Herbert Jhering, "Der Streit um den Sergeanten Grischa," *Börsen Courrier* (April 1, 1930), p. 2 (translated).

2. Paul Fechter, "Grischa als Drama," *Deutsche Allgemeine Zeitung*, (April 1, 1930), p. 2 (translated).

3. Arnold Zweig, *Das Spiel vom Sergeanten Grischa* in *Soldatenspiele* (Berlin, 1956), p. 169 (translated).

4. Zweig, *Das Spiel vom Grischa*, p. 224.

5. Ludwig Sternaux, "Schatten aus dem Gestern, *Lokal Anzeiger*, (April 1, 1930), p. 2.

6. Jhering, *Der Streit um den Grischa.*

7. Kurt Pinthus, "Arnold Zweig's 'Grischa' dramatisiert," *8 Uhr-Abendblatt*, (April 1, 1930), p. 3.

8. Ibid.

9. Fritz Engel, "Der Streit um den Sergeanten Grischa," *Berliner Tageblatt*, (April 1, 1930), p. 4.

10. Arthur Eloesser, "Der Streit um den Sergeanten Grischa," *Vossische Zeitung*, (April 1, 1930), p. 2.

11. The cast included: Aljoscha: Boris Alekin; Fritzke: Friedrich Gnass; Birkholz: Friedrich Ettel; Nikolai: Jarkob Gärtner; Fedka: Stanko Buria; Otto Wild: Erwin Dorow; Man: Martin Kosleck; Dr Wilhemi: Werner Hollmann; Captain: M. R. Ostermann; Brettschneider: Karl Hannemann; and Sacht: Paul Kemp.

12. Wolfgang Storch in Rischbieter, *Bühne und bildende Kunst in XX. Jahrhundert.* (Hannover, 1968), p. 172.

13. Fechter, *Grischa als Drama.*

14. Jhering, *Der Streit um den Grischa.*

15. K. Kn, "Gestern sah man auf der Bühne," *Welt am Abend*, (April 1, 1930), p. 2.

Chapter 9

1. George Grosz, *Briefe 1913-1959.* Herbert Knust, ed. (Hamburg, 1979) pp. 214-15.

2. Ibid., p. 279

3. Ibid., p. 196-98, 200, 202.

4. Ibid., p. 379.

5. Peter Grosz, letter to Andrew DeShong, dated October 9, 1981.

6. George Grosz, *Briefe*, pp. 182-83.

7. George Grosz, *A Little Yes and a Big No.* (New York, 1946) pp. 279-89.

8. Grosz, *Briefe*, pp. 214-15.

9. Ibid. p. 478.

10. The cast included: Preacher: Matthias Klein; Dancing Susannah: Wiet Palar; Singing Susannah: Clare Walmesley; The Elders: Werner Höllein, Harald Sielaff; Fence: Klaus Delonge, Rolfe Hasse; Trees: Roswitha Karwath, Maria Rybarczyk; Maids: Christa Obluda, Rotraut Richtter; Congregation: Renate Laude, Vicky Martius, Eva Meinberg, Christel Willenberg, Heinz Hirsch, Paul Otto Kuster, Georg Gustav Lücke, Julius Volbers; Angel: Klaus Fischer.

11. Quotations are from an article which appeared in July 1948 signed by Quaintance Eaton in the Dance Clipping File of the New York Public Library. The publication is not named in the clipping preserved there and no reference appears in *A Reader's Guide to Periodical Literature*. Other lyrics are in the sheet music published in 1948: Jerome Morross and John Latouche, "I've Got Me," (New York, 1948).

12. Berlin cast of "Willie the Weeper," included: Singing Willie: Ulfried Günther; Dancing Willie: Gert Reinholm; Cocaine Lil: Wiet Palar. The dance-opera was choreographed by Gert Reinholm.

13. The cast of the Berlin "Red Riding Hood" included: Mother Nature: Tatjana Sais; Red Riding Hood: Wiet Palar; Student (Good Humor Man): Gunther Pfitzmann; Wolf: Werner Höllein; Grandmother: Herta Härter; Berman: Harald Sielaff; Clouds: Clare Walmesly, Renate Laude, Vicky Martius; Tree: Harald Sielaff, Georg Gustav Lucke, Heinz Hirsch, Klaus Delonge, Rolf Hasse, Rotraut Richter, Paul Otto Kuster, Julius Volbers, Maria Rybarczyk, Eva Meinberg, Christel Willenberg, Roswith Karwath, Christa Obluda.

14. Walter Kaul, "Die erste Ballade war die beste," *Der Kurier*, (Sept. 23, 1954). Unpaginated clipping from the George Grosz Estate files (translated).

15. Hermann Wanderscheck, "Vier Premieren beim Berlin Festival," *Abendpost* Frankfurt/M (Sept. 29, 1954), unpaginated clipping from George Grosz Estate file (translated).

16. Walter Kaul, "Die erste Ballade."

17. Dora Fehling, "Rotkappchen frisst den Wolf," *Industriekorrespondenzblatt* (Sept. 24, 1954), unpaginated clipping from the files of the George Grosz Estate (translated).

18. *Darmstadter Echo* (Oct. 9, 1954), unpaginated clipping from the files of the George Grosz Estate (translated).

19. Grosz's autobiography was issued in German with an additional chapter that had been omitted in the prior English version. This description of his trip to the Soviet Union in 1922 and his essentially negative reaction to the lack of individual liberties there and to the role of the artist in Soviet society was reprinted as "Russlandreise, 1922," in *Der Monat* (V, 56) pp. 135–152. The Cold War and a clarification of his position *vis à vis* Soviet society were even more directly involved in his caricatures of Soviet totalitarianism for several issues of *Life* in March 1954.

Bibliography

Ashton, Dore. "A Planned Coincidence," *Art in America* LVII, 5 (Sept.-Oct., 1969), pp. 36-47.

Auden, W. H. *The Dyer's Hand.* New York, 1962.

Bab, Julius. *Das Theater der Gegenwart.* Leipzig, 1928.

————. "The Theater in the German Language Area Since the World War," in Thomas H. Dickinson, *The Theater in a Changing Europe.* New York, 1937, pp. 121-178.

Bablet, Denis. *Esthétique générale du décor du théâtre de 1870 à 1914.* Paris, 1965.

Baur, J. I. H. *George Grosz.* New York, 1954.

Béhar, Henri. *Étude sur le théâtre dada et surréaliste.* Paris, 1967.

Bentley, Eric. *Bernard Shaw.* New York, 1957.

Bergman, Gösta M. *Den Moderna Teaterns Genombrott 1890-1925.* Stockholm, 1966.

Bie, Oskar. *Das Theater: Karl Walser.* Berlin, 1912.

Bittner, Herbert, ed. *George Grosz.* introd. Ruth Berenson and Norbert Muhlen. London, 1965.

Boyer, Richard O. "Profiles," *New Yorker.* (November 27, 1943), pp. 32-36, 38, 41-44; (December 4, 1943), pp. 39-44, 46, 48; (December 11, 1943), pp. 37-42, 44.

Brecht, Bertolt, et al. *Theaterarbeit: 6 Aufführungen des Berliner Ensembles.* Dresden, 1952.

Carter, Huntley. *The Theater of Max Reinhardt.* New York, 1914.

Chiarini, Paulo (ed.) *Teatro nella Reppublica di Weimar.* (Roma, 1978).

Corvin, Michel. "Georges Ribemont Dessaignes et le laboratoire Art et Action," *Cahiers Dada—Surréalisme* (I, 1966), pp. 164-65.

Craig, Edward Gordon. *Towards a New Theatre.* New York, 1913.

Dada (Stedeljk Museum Catalog 199). Amsterdam, 1958.

Dada Ausstellung zum 50 Jährigen Jubiläum. Zurich, 1967.

Dada: Monograph of a Movement. ed. Willy Verkauf. New York, 1957.

Dahlback, Bengt. *John Heartfield.* Moderna Museets Utställningskatalog 66. Stockholm, 1967.

Deak, Istvan. *Weimar Germany's Left-Wing Intellectuals: A Political History of the Weltbühne and its Circle.* Berkeley, 1968.

Demange, Camille. "L'Expressionisme allemand et le mouvement révolutionnaire," in *Le Théâtre moderne.* ed. Jean Jacquot. Paris, 1968.

DeShong, Andrew. The Theatrical Designs of George Grosz. Unpublished doctoral diss., Yale, 1970.

Dictionary of Modern Ballet. ed. Francis Gadan, Robert Maillard, and Selma Jean Cohen. New York, 1959.

Die Deutsche Theaterausstellung, Magdeburg, 1927. Magdeburg, 1928.

Dombrow, Sinclair, "The German Babbitt on the Stage," *Vanity Fair* XX, 5 (July, 1923), pp. 65, 96.

Dückers, Alexander. *George Grosz: Das Druckgraphische Werk.* (Frankfurt am Main, 1979).

Ehrenburg, Ilya. "George Grosz," *Blätter für der Reinhardt Bühnen, 1929-30.* ed. Hans Rothe. Vol. 6.

Eisner, Lotte H. *L'Écran démoniaque, influence de Max Reinhardt et de l'expressionisme.* Paris, 1952.

Esslin, Martin. *Bertolt Brecht.* New York, 1969.

———. *The Theatre of the Absurd.* 2nd ed. Garden City, 1969.

Eyck, Erich. *A History of the Weimar Republic.* 2 vols. Cambridge, 1963-67.

Fischel, Oskar. *Das Moderne Bühnenbild.* Berlin, 1923.

Flaubert, Gustav. *Oeuvres completes,* XLIV Theatre. Paris, 1910.

Fuerst, S. J. and Walter Rene Hume. *Twentieth Century Stage Decoration.* 2 vols. London, 1928; New York, 1967.

Garten, H. P. *Modern German Drama.* New York, 1962.

Gay, Peter. *Weimar Culture: the Outsider as Insider.* New York, 1968.

George Grosz, 1893-1959. Catalog of exhibition, Forum and Thaw Galleries, New York. introd. Hans Hess. New York, 1963.

Goll, Iwan and Claire Goll. *Iwan Goll-Claire Goll Briefe.* Berlin, 1966.

Goll, Iwan. *Methusalem or the Eternal Bourgeois.* trans. Arthur S. Wensinger and Clinton J. Atkinson. *Plays for a New Theater.* New York, 1966.

Gombrich, E. H. *Art and Illusion.* Third Printing, Second Edition. Princeton, 1969.

Gorelik, Mordecai. *New Theatres for Old.* Second Edition. New York, 1962.

Grimm, Reinhold. *Episches Theater.* Köln, 1966.

Gröning, Karl and Werner Kliess, *Friedrichs Theaterlexikon.* ed. Henning Rischbieter. Hannover, 1969.

Gropius, Walter. *The Theater of the Bauhaus.* ed. Arthur S. Wensinger. Middletown, Connecticut, 1969.

Grosz, George. "Le Beau Monde," *La Revue du Cinéma* (August 1, 1931), pp. 112-17.

———. *Briefe. 1913-1959,* ed. by Herbert Knust, (Hamburg, 1979).

———. *George Grosz: dessins et aquarelles.* Exhibition Catalog, Galerie Claude Bernard. Paris, 1966.

———. *Deutschland über Alles.* ed. Ulrich Becher. Rome, 1963.

———. *Ecce Homo.* Introd. Lee Revens. New York, 1965.

———. *Das Gesicht der herrschenden Klasse.* Berlin, 1924.

———. *Die Gezeichneten.* Berlin, 1928.

———. *Hintergrund.* Berlin, 1928.

———. *A Little Yes and a Big No.* trans. Lola Sachs Dorin. New York, 1946.

———. *Ohne Hemmung.* Catalog, Galerie Nierendorf, Berlin. Berlin, 1962.

———. "Russlandreise, 1922," *Der Monat* V, 56 (May, 1954), pp. 135-52.

———. *Der Spiesser-Spiegel.* Dresden, 1925.

Gussmann, Hans. *Theatergebäude.* 2 vols. Berlin, 1954.

Hasek, Jaroslav. *The Good Soldier Schweik.* trans. Paul Selver. New York, 1930.

Hecht, Werner. *Brechts Weg zum epischen Theater.* Berlin, 1962.

Hellberg, Martin, *Bühne und Film.* Berlin, 1955.

Herald, Heinz. *Das grosse Schauspielhaus.* Berlin, 1920.

Herzfelde, Wieland. *John Heartfield: Leben und Werk.* Leipzig, 1962.

Hess, Hans. *George Grosz.* N.Y. (1974).

Hildebrandt, Hans. *Oskar Schlemmer.* Munich, 1952.

Hollaender, Friedrich. *Von Kopf bis Fuss.* Munich, 1965.

Hosch, Rudolf. *Kabarett von Gestern,* I, *1900-33.* Berlin, 1967.

Huelsenbeck, Richard. *Dada Almanach.* New York, 1966.

Hugnet, Georges. *L'Aventure dada, 1916-1922.* Paris, 1957.

Innes, C. D. Erwin Piscator's Political Theatre, The Development of Modern German Drama. Cambridge, 1972.

Jacobsohn, Siegfried. *Das Jahr der Bühne, 1920/21.* Berlin, 1921.

————. *Max Reinhardt*. Berlin, 1910.

Janssen, Franzjosef. *Bühnenbild und bildende Künstler*. Frankfurt, 1957.

Jhering, Herbert. "Piscator," *Enciclopedia dello Spettacolo*. 9 vols. Rome, 1961. VIII, pp. 186–90.

————. *Reinhardt, Jessner, Piscator oder Klassikertod?*. Berlin, 1929.

————. *Von Reinhardt bis Brecht*. 3 vols. Berlin, 1961.

Kaiser, Georg. *Kanzlist Krehler*. Potsdam, 1922.

————. *Nebeneinander*. Potsdam, 1923.

Kenworthy, B. J. *George Kaiser*, Oxford, 1957.

Kerr, Alfred. *Die Welt im Drama*. Köln, 1964.

Kessler, Harry. *Aus den Tagebüchern 1918–1937*. ed. Wolfgang Pfeiffer-Belli. Munich, 1965.

————. "In the Twenties," *Encounter*. transl. Sarah Gainam (XXIX, 1–3, July–Sept., 1967), pp. 3–17, 7–17, 17–28.

Kindermann, Heinz. *Theatergeschichte Europas*. 8 vols. VIII. Salzburg, 1968.

Knust, Herbert and Hedy Landman. *Theatrical Drawings and Watercolors by George Grosz Exhibition Catalog*. Busch Reisinger Museum, Harvard, 1973.

Kortner, Fritz. *Aller Tage Abend*. Munich, 1959.

Kosch, Wilhelm. *Deutsches Theaterlexikon*. Klagenfurt, 1951– (ongoing).

Kracauer, Siegfried. *From Caligari to Hitler*. Princeton, 1947.

Kranich, Friedrich. *Bühnentechnik der Gegenwart*. 2 vols. Munich, I, 1929, II, 1933.

Krell, Max, ed. *Das Deutsche Theater der Gegenwart*. Munich, 1923.

Latouche, John and Jerome Moross. "I've Got Me." New York, 1948.

MacGowan, Kenneth and Robert Edmond Jones. *Continental Stagecraft*. New York, 1922.

Mann, Golo. *Deutsche Geschichte 1919–1945*. Fifth Edition. Frankfurt, 1964.

Mann, Klaus. *The Turning Point*. New York, 1942.

Mehring, Walter. *Berlin Dada*. Zurich, 1959.

————. *George Grosz, Thirty Drawings and Watercolors*. New York, 1944.

————. *The Lost Library: The Autobiography of a Culture*. London, 1951.

————. *Das neue Ketzerbrevier*. Köln, 1962.

————. *Neues Ketzerbrevier Balladen und Songs*. Munich, 1966.

————. *Der Zeitpuls fliegt*. Hamburg, 1958.

Meisel, Martin. *Shaw and the Nineteenth-Century Theater*. Princeton, 1963.

Melchinger, Siegfried, and Rosemarie Clausen. *Schauspieler*. Hannover, 1965.

————. and Gottfried von Einem. *Caspar Neher*. Hannover, 1966.

von Meyerinck, Hubert. *Meine berühmten Freundinnen: Erinnerungen*. Düsseldorf, 1967.

Mildenberger, Marianne. "Die Anwendung von Projektion und Film als Mittel szenischer Gestaltung." Unpub. Diss. Köln, 1958.

Motherwell, Robert. *The Dada Painters and Poets: An Anthology*. New York, 1951.

Moussinac, Léon. *Tendances nouvelles de théâtre*. Paris, 1931.

Naylor, Gillian. *The Bauhaus*. New York, 1968.

Niessen, Carl. *Max Reinhardt und seine Bühnenbildner*. Köln, 1958.

Orlik, Emil. *Schauspielerbildnisse aus der Büchse der Pandora von Frank Wedekind*. Berlin, 1919.

Patterson, Michael. *Revolution in German Theater. 1900–1933*. Boston, 1981.

Petr, Pavel. *Hasek's "Schwejk" in Deutschland*. Berlin, 1963.

Pierre, Jose. *Le Futurisme et le dadaisme*. Lausanne, 1966.

Piscator, Erwin. "Zu meiner Inszenierung von Zech 'Das trunkene Schiff' in der Berliner Volksbühne," *Das Kunstblatt* (July, 1926), pp. 273–77.

————. *The Political Theatre*. New York, 1978.

————. *Das politische Theater*. Berlin, 1929.

————. *Das politische Theater*. ed. and rev. Felix Gasbarra. Hamburg, 1963.

————. *Le Théâtre politique*, trans. Arthur Adamov. Paris, 1962.

Ray, Marcel. *George Grosz*. Paris, 1927.

Reinhardt, Max. *Ausgewählte Briefe, Reden und Szenen aus Regiebüchern.* ed. Franz Hadamowsky. Wien, 1963.

Richter, Hans. *Dada Profiles*. Zurich, 1961.

————. *Dada Art and Anti-Art*. trans. David Britt. London, 1966.

Ripellino, Angelo Maria and Paulo Chiarini. "Projezione," *Enciclopedia dello Spettaculo*. 9 vols. Rome, 1961. VIII, pp. 518–20.

Rischbieter, Henning. *Art and the Stage in the 20th Century*. transl. Michael Bullock, cat. Andreas Schroeder. Greenwich, 1969.

————. *Bühne und bildende Kunst in XX. Jahrhundert*. Hannover, 1968.

————. "Piscator und seine Zeit," *Theater Heute* (May, 1966), pp. 56–61.

Rubin, William S. *Dada and Surrealist Art*. New York, 1969.

————. *Dada, Surrealism and Their Heritage*. New York, 1968.

Rühle, Günther. *Theater für die Republik*. Frankfurt, 1967.

Rühle, Jürgen. *Theater und Revolution*. Munich, 1963.

Sayler, Oliver M. *Max Reinhardt and his Theatre*. New York, 1924.

Scheffer, Herbert. "Forderungen an einen Bühnenbilder," *Das Theater* VII, 12, p. 279.

Schifferli, Peter, ed. *Als Dada begann*. Zurich, 1957.

Schlemmer, Oskar. *Briefe und Tagebücher*. Munich, 1958.

————. *The Letters and Diaries of Oskar Schlemmer*. ed. Tut Schlemmer. trans. Krishna Winston, Middletown (1972).

Schneede, Uwe M. *George Grosz, John Heartfield*. Exhibition catalog, Wurttembergerisch Kunsteverein, Stuttgart, 1969.

————. *George Grosz, His Life and Work*. New York, 1979.

Schoenberner, Franz. *Confessions of a European Intellectual*. New York, 1946.

————. *The Inside Story of an Outsider*. New York, 1949.

Schöne, Günther. "Die Technik in den Inszenierungen Erwin Piscators," *Bühnentechnische Rundschau* (Aug., 1966), pp. 9–13.

Schulz, Eugen. "Die Inszenierung von Georg Kaisers 'Nebeneinander' im Stadttheater M. Gladbach," *Die Scene* XVI (1926–1927), p. 179.

Schwarz, Arturo. *Cinquant' anni a Dada*. Milan, 1966.

Shaw, George Bernard. *Complete Plays with Prefaces*. 6 vols. New York, 1962–1963.

Singer, Hans W. *Zeichnungen von Emil Orlik*. Leipzig, 1914.

Sokel, Walter H. *Anthology of German Expressionist Drama: A Prelude to the Absurd*. New York, 1963.

Die Spielpläne Max Reinhardt 1905–1930. ed. Franz Horch. Munich, 1930.

Stern, Ernst. *Bühnenbilder bei Max Reinhardt*. Berlin, 1955.

Sternheim, Carl. *Der Kandidat*. Leipzig, 1914.

Toller, Ernst. *I Was a German*. New York, 1930.

————. *Seven Plays*. trans. Edward Crankshaw. New York, 1936.

————. *Die Wandlung: das Ringen eines Menschen*. Potsdam, 1924.

"Unterhaltung zwischen Ohnesorge und Grosz," *Ausnahmezustand: eine Anthologie aus Weltbühne und Tagebuch*. ed. Wolfgang Weyrauch. Munich, 1966. pp. 209–18.

Walser, Karl. *Das Theater*. Berlin, 1912.

Weimarer Republik. collective work of Kunstamt Kreuzberg and Inst. für Theaterwissenschaft Köln, Berlin, 1977.

West, Richard. "George Grosz: Figure for Yvan Goll's Methusalem," *Bulletin of the Cleveland Museum of Art* (April, 1968), pp. 90–93.

Willet, John. *The Theatre of Erwin Piscator*. N.Y. (1979).

————. *The Theatre of Bertolt Brecht*. 3rd ed. New York, 1968.

————. *Art and Politics in the Weimar Period. The New Sobriety, 1917–1933*. N.Y., 1978.

Zech, Paul. "Prinzipielle Bemerkungen zu der szenischen Ballade 'Das trunkene Schiff.'" *Die Scene* XVI, 6, pp. 175–77.
_____. *Das trunkene Schiff: eine szenische Ballade*. Leipzig, n.d.
Zivier, Georg. *Berlin und der Tanz*. Berlin, 1968.
Znamenacek, Wolfgang. *Kulissen, Sternoffizin*. Augsburg, 1958.
Zweig, Arnold. *The Case of Sergeant Grischa*. transl. Eric Sutton. New York, 1928.
_____. "Das Spiel von Sergeanten Grischa," in *Soldatenspiele*. Berlin, 1956.
Zweig, Stefan. *The World of Yesterday*. New York, 1943.

The following newspapers and periodicals were consulted primarily for reviews:

Der Abend
Abendpost, Frankfurt/M
8-Uhr Abendblatt
Allgemeine Zeitung, Stuttgart
Der Autor
Berliner Börsen-Courier
Berliner Lokal-Anzeiger
Berliner Stimme
Berliner Tageblatt
Berlin Nacht-depesche
Berlin Weltspiegel-Anzeigen
BZ am Mittag
Der Dada
Die Dame
Darmstädter Echo
Deutsche Rundschau
Duisburger General-Anzeiger
Frankfurter Nachtausgabe
Frankfurter Rundschau
Frankfurter Zeitung
Freiheit
Hamburger Anzeiger

Industriekorrespondenzblatt
Der Kurier
Life
Das literarische Echo
Die lustige Blätter
Neue Jugend
Die Neue Zeitung
New York Times
Die Pleite
Rheinische Post
Die rote Fahne
Saturday Review
Spandauer Volksblatt
Stuttgarter Nachrichter
Der Tagerspiegel
Vorwärts
Vossische Zeitung
Die Welt, Hamburg
Welt am Abend
Die Weltbühne
Die Woche
Die Zeit

Index